# WHAT YOUR COLLEAGUES ARE S

MW00580989

*Yet another superb Nottingham Learning Pit publicatio... ~~~~~, yet accessible, practical yet thought-provoking, this book lays out comprehensive lesson ideas, built around searching questions, which take students through cognitive conflict to deep understanding of secondary English contexts.*

**Shirley Clarke**
Formative Assessment Expert

*The potential of this book is paramount; a valuable resource for any secondary language arts classroom.*

**Miriam A. DeCock**
Language Arts Instructor: Secondary & Adult Education
Wadena Deer Creek ISD
Wadena, MN

*This book provides a fresh, engaging approach to traditional texts, from poetry to classics like Romeo and Juliet and Of Mice and Men. The constructive approach fosters students' ability to form and support opinions and inferences, supported by text.*

**Kathleen Swift**
English teacher
Newtown High School
Sandy Hook, CT

*The lessons included in this text are strong examples that I would recommend to any teacher seeking to guide students through the 'Learning Pit' and engage students in critical thinking based upon textual analysis.*

**Audrey L. Harper**
Reading/Writing Consultant for Warren County Schools
Warren County Public Schools
Bowling Green, KY

*The authors have provided a pragmatic teacher resource bridging the concepts of Challenging Learning to instructional implementation in context! For some, it will take the guesswork out of creating a lesson that puts students 'in the Learning Pit'. For others, this text will be influential in sparking their creativity for systematic lesson design.*

**Kevin R. Kirkwood**
School Improvement Coordinator
Genesee Valley Educational Partnership (BOCES)
Le Roy, NY

*This is an excellent resource for any teacher seeking to develop the quality of dialogue in their classroom. It's a very practical resource, which neatly bridges the gap between theory and practical application. Imaginative use of these ideas will enable teachers to offer challenging and engaging learning experiences for students and develop their capacity for creativity and critical thinking. I would whole-heartedly recommend this excellent, highly readable addition to the 'Challenging Learning' library.*

**Geoff Moorcroft**
Director of Education, Isle of Man

The Nottinghams have written a must-read, practical implementation guide for any ELA teacher considering integrating Challenging Learning into their classroom. This book provides ELA teachers with countless strategies and a systematic approach to lesson planning that will move students to deeper understanding of conceptual ideas through dialogue and exploratory talk. This text is the perfect 'how to' companion to Nottingham's previous publications. Read this book and walk away with the confidence to effectively and efficiently plan to move students in and out of 'the Learning Pit' on a regular basis.

**Sarah Callahan**
Director of School Improvement
Genesee Valley Educational Partnership

The work of James and Jill Nottingham, along with all of their colleagues at Challenging Learning, has finally provided the 'what next' in education to support deep and engaging learning for all students. Within their series of Challenging Learning books, including Learning Challenge Lessons for ELA Students, educators are able to take the key ideas within Challenging Learning and the Learning Pit, and put them into practice in a practical way. Every secondary ELA teacher needs to get this resource in their hands!

**Garth Larson**
Co-Founder and Consultant with FIRST Educational Resources (USA)

The Learning Challenge Lessons book is brilliant for improved learning on several levels. First of all, it provides you with an insight on how to design for deeper learning for students, by role-modelling lots of examples of how to use and 'travel through' The Learning Pit. Second, it helps you as an adult to develop a common language for and a better understand of learning in general. And last, but not least, it challenges your students' thinking (and perhaps yours as well), and therefore their overall learning skills.

**Ingelin Burkeland**
KS-Konsulent AS

This book is a must for secondary teachers searching for strategies to guide adolescents through creating and replicating the thrill experienced from learning. If you are hungry to activate your students to embark on a challenging journey – from being in a state of cognitive dissonance until progressing to the point of 'EUREKA! I'VE GOT IT!' – then the Nottinghams have answers sure to satisfy your craving!

**Tara Noe**
Instructional Coach

Guiding students through the Learning Pit to promote challenge, dialogue, productive struggle, critical thinking and a growth mindset has just become easier thanks to the Challenging Learning Team led by Jill and James Nottingham. This book has concrete lessons and activities connected to great works of literature to guide students from surface-level knowledge to deep understanding – with an overarching goal of transfer. The best part, the activities and lessons presented in this book can be adapted to any complex, engaging text!

**Paul Bloomberg, Founder & Chief Learning Officer**
The Core Collaborative Student-Centered Learning Network

As someone who is continually striving to improve the quality of learning experienced by young people I am delighted to see the publication of this book. Another title from Challenging Learning packed full with straightforward practical strategies, outlined clearly for the teacher and applied to learning contexts so that anyone can pick them up and transfer them to their own setting. Just what we need to engage young people and enthuse their teachers in learning. More challenge, more learning!

**Archie Bathgate**
Headteacher, Brechin High School

*This is an extremely useful and relevant resource, which combines a wealth of practical activities and strategies with a comprehensive theoretical explanation of how thinking is deepened using the learning challenge. Since using this knowledge and approach I have seen an improved pedagogy with my teaching staff and a resilient approach to learning with my pupils. I recommend this book to any teacher regardless of their subject or teaching phase.*

**Jill Harland**
Headteacher, Brudenell Primary School

*21st Century learning easily comes alive in this latest resource by Jill Nottingham et al. Collaboration, cooperation, creativity and critical thinking will abound in your classroom as you lead your students into 'The Pit' with these engaging ELA lesson ideas. Combining Challenging Learning's research on positive mindset with student growth through productive struggle, these 20 carefully curated lessons include everything from a lesson plan to student materials. Brilliant! This resource is a teacher's dream.*

**Karen Nguyen**
33-year classroom veteran
Kindergarten, The Downtown School
Bakersfield, California, USA

*As someone whose teaching was fundamentally transformed by the Learning Pit and Challenging Learning concepts I was hugely impressed by this new book. James and Jill have taken a highly effective series of concepts and honed them to another level. As well as being an effective manual on techniques backed up with the pedagogical theory that supports them, it also includes a huge number of activities linked to core texts from the new GCSE curriculum. A well-researched piece carefully constructed to be practical, informative and instantly applicable.*

**Barry Dunn**
Teacher

# CHALLENGING LEARNING SERIES

**The Learning Challenge: How to Guide Your Students Through the Learning Pit to Achieve Deeper Understanding**
by James Nottingham

**Challenging Mindset: Why a Growth Mindset Makes a Difference in Learning – and What to Do When It Doesn't**
by James Nottingham and Bosse Larsson

**Challenging Learning Through Dialogue: Strategies to Engage Your Students and Develop Their Language of Learning**
by James Nottingham, Jill Nottingham and Martin Renton

**Challenging Learning Through Feedback: How to Get the Type, Tone and Quality of Feedback Right Every Time**
by James Nottingham and Jill Nottingham

**Challenging Learning Through Questioning**
by James Nottingham and Martin Renton

**Learning Challenge Lessons, Primary: 20 Lessons to Guide Young Learners Through the Learning Pit**
by Jill Nottingham and James Nottingham with Mark Bollom, Joanne Nugent and Lorna Pringle

**Learning Challenge Lessons, Secondary English Language Arts**
by Jill Nottingham, James Nottingham and Mark Bollom with Joanne Nugent and Lorna Pringle

**Learning Challenge Lessons, Secondary Mathematics**
by Jill Nottingham and James Nottingham with Mark Bollom, Joanne Nugent and Lorna Pringle

# LEARNING CHALLENGE
# LESSONS

## Secondary English Language Arts

# LEARNING CHALLENGE
# LESSONS

## Secondary English Language Arts

20 Lessons to Guide Students
Through the Learning Pit

By Jill Nottingham, James Nottingham and
Mark Bollom

With Joanne Nugent and Lorna Pringle

CORWIN
A SAGE Publishing Company

FOR INFORMATION:

Corwin

A SAGE Company

2455 Teller Road

Thousand Oaks, California 91320

(800) 233-9936

www.corwin.com

SAGE Publications Ltd.

1 Oliver's Yard

55 City Road

London, EC1Y 1SP

United Kingdom

SAGE Publications India Pvt. Ltd.

B 1/I 1 Mohan Cooperative Industrial Area

Mathura Road, New Delhi 110 044

India

SAGE Publications Asia-Pacific Pte. Ltd.

18 Cross Street #10-10/11/12

China Square Central

Singapore 048423

Acquisitions Editor: Ariel Curry

Development Editor: Desirée A. Bartlett

Associate Content Development Editor: Jessica Vidal

Production Editor: Tori Mirsadjadi

Copy Editor: Rosemary Campbell

Typesetter: Hurix Digital

Proofreader: Diana Chambers

Indexer: Beth Nauman-Montana

Cover and Interior Designer: Janet Kiesel

Marketing Manager: Margaret O'Connor

ISBN 978-1-5443-3052-5

This book is printed on acid-free paper.

19 20 21 22 23 10 9 8 7 6 5 4 3 2 1

# CONTENTS

# PART II: THE LESSON IDEAS

# REFERENCES

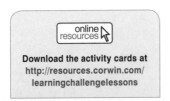

**Download the activity cards at
http://resources.corwin.com/
learningchallengelessons**

# LIST OF FIGURES

# INDEX OF CONCEPTS

# ACKNOWLEDGEMENTS

The authors would also like to thank the following people for their support and suggestions:

Ariel Curry
Elaine Davies
Dan Henderson
Andrew Parsons
Laura Taylor
Phil Thompson

The authors can be contacted through www.challenginglearning.com

# PUBLISHER'S ACKNOWLEDGEMENTS

Corwin gratefully acknowledges the contributions of the following reviewers:

Helene Alalouf
Education Consultant
Various NYC schools
NY

Claudia A. Danna
Adjunct Professor, Complementary Observer for Teacher Evaluation and
Curriculum Support
Sacred Heart University/Griswold Public Schools/Canterbury Public Schools
Griswold, CT

Miriam A. DeCock
Language Arts Instructor: Secondary & Adult Education
Wadena Deer Creek ISD
Wadena, MN

Audrey L. Harper
Reading/Writing Consultant for Warren County Schools
Warren County Public Schools
Bowling Green, KY

Kevin R. Kirkwood
School Improvement Coordinator
Genesee Valley Educational Partnership (BOCES)
Le Roy, NY

Rebecca Rupert
9–12 English Language Arts, Teacher
Bloomington Graduation School
Bloomington, IN

Kathleen Swift
English Teacher
Newtown High School
Sandy Hook, CT

# ABOUT THE AUTHORS

**Jill Nottingham**'s background is in teaching, leadership and consultancy. She has been a teacher and leader in kindergartens and schools in some of the more socially deprived areas of North East England. During that time, she developed many approaches to teaching children how to learn that are still being used in schools and taught in universities today.

Jill has also trained with Edward de Bono at the University of Malta, and has studied for a Master's degree in Education with the University of Newcastle.

Jill now leads Challenging Learning's pre-school and primary school consultancy. She has written many of the Challenging Learning teaching materials, has edited the others, and is currently writing three books for schools and two books for pre-schools. In amongst this she finds time to be the mother of three gorgeous children!

**James Nottingham** is co-founder and director of Challenging Learning, a group of companies with 30 employees in six countries. His passion is in transforming the most up-to-date research into strategies that really work in the classroom. He is regarded by many as one of the most engaging, thought-provoking and inspirational speakers in education.

His first book, *Challenging Learning*, was published in 2010 and has received widespread critical acclaim. Since then, he has written six books for teachers, leaders, support staff and parents. These books share the best research and practice connected with learning, dialogue, feedback, the Learning Pit, early years education and growth mindset.

Before training to be a teacher, James worked on a pig farm, in the chemical industry, for the American Red Cross, and as a teaching assistant in a school for deaf children. At university, he gained a first-class honours degree in Education (a major turnaround after having failed miserably at school). He then worked as a teacher and leader in primary and secondary schools in the UK before co-founding an award-winning, multi-million-pound regeneration project supporting education, public and voluntary organisations across North East England.

Skolvärlden (Swedish Teaching Union) describes James as 'one of the most talked about names in the world of school development' and the *Observer* newspaper in the UK listed him among the Future 500 – a 'definitive list of the UK's most forward-thinking and brightest innovators'.

**Mark Bollom** is a writer and consultant with Challenging Learning. He has a background in primary, secondary, tertiary and special needs education. He has worked for Challenging Learning since 2015 and has contributed to the company's extensive bank of Learning Challenge resources. Mark's role also supports and develops the wider writing team within the company.

In addition, Mark also works as a Challenging Learning consultant in schools, colleges and city-wide municipalities, promoting stronger learning through the long-term project work the company undertakes. As part of this work he monitors the effectiveness and impact of the resources that Challenging Learning produces, trialling and observing these in action.

# ABOUT THE CONTRIBUTORS

**Joanne Nugent** is a Product Resource Developer and part of the Product Development team at Challenging Learning where she enjoys writing and editing many of their classroom resources. She is passionate about creating resources that engage and challenge students, enabling them to realise their potential and develop a love of learning.

Joanne's background is in teaching, leading and consultancy, working with young people across the 11–18 age group. Her work has featured in many national and international publications, including the highly successful *Thinking through History* resource book.

**Lorna Pringle** is a Product Resource Developer at Challenging Learning, working on creating stimulating resources to enhance classroom practice. Lorna is a highly successful teacher of English at secondary level who has over 15 years' experience of teaching, including in schools and colleges, teaching adult education and working with children with special educational needs.

She currently splits her time between working for Challenging Learning and teaching children unable to be schooled in mainstream schools.

# THE LANGUAGE OF LEARNING

**Here are some of the terms we have used in this book.**

**Cognitive conflict:** Cognitive conflict is created when contradictions are identified and options examined. It is the disagreement between two or more of the ideas or opinions a person holds concurrently. It is this conflict or 'wobble', which causes more reflection and the questioning of assumptions.

**Concept:** A general idea that groups things together according to accepted characteristics.

**Construct:** Shorthand for stage three of the Learning Challenge in which participants construct meaning by connecting, explaining and examining patterns and relationships.

**Cumulative talk:** Talk that is characterised by repetitions, confirmations and elaborations.

**Dialogue:** Dialogue is conversation and enquiry. Dialogue combines the sociability of conversation with the skills of framing questions and constructing answers.

**Discussion:** The action or process of talking about something and exchanging ideas.

**Disputational talk:** Talk that is critical of individuals (and their ideas), focuses on differences, is competitive and is all about being seen to 'win'.

**Enquiry:** A process of questioning ideas, information and assumptions and of augmenting knowledge, resolving doubt, or solving a problem.

**Eureka:** Taken from the Greek word for 'I found it', the eureka moment is reached as students climb out of the pit with a new sense of clarity and understanding.

**Exploratory talk:** Talk that is characterised by longer exchanges, use of questions, reflection, explanation and speculation.

**IRE:** The 'IRE' structure of classroom interaction is: teacher *Initiation* – student *Response* – teacher *Evaluation*. Teachers use this most common pattern of classroom talk to ensure that pupils remember what they already know. This is not what we mean by dialogue.

**Knowledge:** Acquaintance with facts, truths or principles. Generally considered to be a step removed from understanding, which is when someone is able to relate, explain and evaluate.

**Language of reasoning:** The words, phrases and concepts that structure thinking, discussion or writing of any complexity. They help people think about everything else.

**Learning intention:** A learning intention describes what students should know, understand or be able to do by the end of the lesson or series of lessons.

**Metacognition:** Literally meaning 'thinking about thinking', meta-cognition is an important part of dialogue. It encourages students to think about the way in which they are thinking, how they are using the strategies, and how they might improve for next time.

**Pit:** A metaphor to identify the state of confusion a person feels when holding two or more conflicting thoughts or opinions in their mind at the same time.

**Reflection:** Giving serious thought or consideration to a thought, idea or response.

**Skills:** The abilities to carry out those processes necessary for gaining understanding, completing tasks or performing in any given context.

**Success criteria:** Summarise the key steps or ingredients students need to accomplish the learning intention. They encompass the main things to do, include or focus on.

**Understanding:** The mental process of a person who comprehends. It includes an ability to explain cause, effect and significance, and to understand patterns and how they relate to each other.

**Wobble:** User-friendly term to describe a state of cognitive conflict.

**Zone of Proximal Development:** Used by Lev Vygotsky to describe the zone between actual and potential development.

# PART I:
# SETTING
# THE
# SCENE

# Preparing to Use the Lesson Ideas

## 1.0 INTRODUCTION

This book shares a range of excellent lesson ideas to help you guide your students through the Learning Pit. Here you will find guidance for setting up and running lessons around topics as thought-provoking as exploration, language, fairness, time and friendship. Each lesson has a set of resources to use with your students as well as recommended activities to make progress from first thoughts to deep **understanding**.

To make the most of each lesson idea in this book, we recommend that you also read the following books.

### The Learning Challenge

*The Learning Challenge* (Nottingham, 2017) describes the theory and practice of guiding students through the 'Learning Pit'. It covers everything from background to rationale, from establishing a learning culture to techniques for challenging, motivating and guiding students from surface level **knowledge** to deeper understanding. It shows how contradictions and uncertainties can be used to think more deeply, and how being 'in the pit' makes learning more rigorous and engaging.

### Challenging Learning Through Dialogue

*Challenging Learning Through Dialogue* (Nottingham, Nottingham and Renton, 2017) shares some of the best strategies for using **dialogue** to enhance learning. It includes examples of the strategies used in the lessons within this book and Philosophy for Children (P4C) techniques to help students learn how to think, how to be reasonable, how to make moral decisions, and how to understand another person's point of view.

These two books will give you a deeper insight into how to use the lesson ideas in this book more effectively. The main sections to read before trying out any of the lesson ideas in this book include the following.

### The Learning Challenge

An introduction to the Learning Challenge: Chapter 1

1. Values and ground rules for engaging students: Sections 3.1, 3.2 and 3.4

2. Identifying concepts: Sections 4.2, 4.2.1 and 4.3

3. Creating and selecting questions: Sections 4.4 and 4.5

4. Generating cognitive conflict: Chapter 5

5. Constructing answers and the **'eureka'** moment: Sections 6.1, 6.4 and 6.5

6. Reviewing and **metacognition** techniques: Sections 7.1 and 7.2

The difference between dialogue and **discussion**: Sections 2.0 and 2.6

1. Creating the right environment for dialogue: Sections 3.1, 3.2 and 3.3

2. Using dialogue to develop reasoning and reasonableness: Chapter 4

3. Groupings and ground rules: Chapter 5

4. Opinion Lines and Corners: Sections 7.2 and 7.3

5. How to run a Mystery: Sections 8.1, 8.2, 8.4 and 8.6

6. Philosophy for Children: Sections 11.1, 11.2 and 11.4

Once you have read these sections, you will be in a much better position to make the most of the lesson ideas in this book. For now, though, here are some brief notes to get you started.

# 1.1 THE LEARNING CHALLENGE

James Nottingham created the Learning Challenge in 2003 as a way to help his students think and talk about learning. It is rather like a child-friendly representation of Vygotsky's **Zone of Proximal Development** (1978) in that it describes the move from actual to potential understanding. Since its inception, the Learning Challenge has captured the imagination of educators, students and their parents. It has featured in many periodicals, articles and books, and it now appears on classroom walls around the world.

The Learning Challenge promotes challenge, dialogue and a growth mindset. It offers participants the opportunity to think and talk about their own learning. It encourages a depth of **enquiry** that moves learners from surface-level knowledge to deep understanding. It encourages an exploration of causation and impact; an interpretation and comparison of meaning; a classification and sequencing of detail; and a recognition and analysis of pattern. It builds learners' resilience, determination and curiosity. And it nurtures a love of learning.

At the heart of the Learning Challenge is 'the **pit**'. A person could be said to be 'in the pit' when they are in a state of **cognitive conflict** – that is to say, when a person has two or more ideas that make sense to them, but when compared side by side they appear to be in conflict with each other. Each of the lesson plans in this book are designed to create that exact situation, so that your students need to think more deeply about the topic.

Examples of the sort of cognitive conflicts you will find in this book include:

- We are all responsible for our own actions, and yet sometimes we act because we are following orders or instructions from others (Lesson 1: Who was responsible for the death of William in Mary Shelley's *Frankenstein*?).

- Monstrous people are born that way, but monstrous people develop in response to the conditions around them (Lesson 4: Was Heathcliff a monster?).

- Love is impossible to define and yet everyone knows what love is (Lesson 11: Is Romeo really in love?).

- We are free to make choices, but our choices are influenced (Lesson 16: Does the poem 'The Road Not Taken' show us how to make the right choice?).

- Happiness is a choice, but happiness is also a spontaneous response to events (Lesson 18: Did Anne Frank experience happiness?).

- A great speech can only persuade us of something we want to believe, but perhaps a great speech can make us think we want to believe something (Lesson 19: Why was Winston Churchill's speech effective?).

When your students think through these or other examples of cognitive conflict, then they will find themselves 'in the pit'.

It is important to note that learners are *not* in the pit when they have *no* idea. The pit represents moving beyond a single, basic idea into the situation of having multiple ideas that are as yet unsorted. This happens when a learner purposefully explores inconsistencies, exceptions and contradictions in their own or others' thinking so as to discover a richer, more complex understanding. That is why each of the lesson ideas aims to move participants out of their comfort zone. This is a deliberate and strategic objective. It is neither incidental nor casual. It is not something that happens parenthetically. The very purpose of the lessons is to get your students into the pit (and back out again)!

## Timing and Pacing

To achieve this, we recommend that you use the four steps of the Learning Challenge. You don't have to include all of these steps in just one lesson, and, indeed, you may not be able to because of time. We have included recommendations for each stage, but we have not said how you might time each step because this would depend on a number of variables, such as the needs of your students, their prior learning and your context or

▶ **Figure 1.1: The Learning Challenge**

setting. For example, you might wish to set the scene and cover stage 1 before the lesson and you might like to invite your students to complete stage 4 at a later date – perhaps for homework or within informal small-group extension activities. You might find that you need (or want) to spend longer exploring the **concept** and creating cognitive conflict around that concept through extending the questioning and developing the dialogue that stems from that questioning. It really is up to you! Nothing is set in stone – which is why we have put them forward as lesson 'ideas' rather than lesson 'plans'.

The four steps of the Learning Challenge are as follows.

## Stage 1: Concept

The lesson activities begin by familiarising your students with the underlying concepts. It is not necessary for all participants to understand all the concepts. So long as *some* of your students have *some* understanding of one or more of the concepts then the lesson activities should work well.

## Stage 2: Conflict

The next stage is to create some cognitive conflict around one or more of the concepts. The recommended questions associated with each lesson plan should help you achieve this, as should the structured activities. Remember that the key to the Learning Challenge is to get your students 'into the pit' by creating cognitive conflict in their minds. This deliberate creation of a dilemma is what makes the Learning Challenge such a good model for challenge and enquiry, reasoning and reasonableness, and is precisely what each of the lesson ideas is designed to achieve.

## Stage 3: Construct

After exploring the concepts for a while (and we're being purposefully ambiguous by saying 'for a while' because it depends on context) your students will begin to make links and **construct** meaning. They will do this by examining options, connecting ideas together and explaining cause and effect. Often (though not always) this leads them to a sense of 'eureka' in which they find new clarity. Each lesson idea includes some recommended activities to help them reach this eureka moment by 'climbing out of the pit'.

## Stage 4: Consider

After achieving a sense of **eureka,** your students should reflect on their learning journey. They can do this by considering *how* they progressed from simplistic ideas (stage 1), to the identification of more complex and conflicting ideas (stage 2), through to a deeper understanding of how all these ideas interrelate to each other (stage 3). Now at stage 4, they can think about the best ways to relate and apply their new understanding to different contexts.

### Lesson Ideas Format

In Chapter 2, you'll find a description of the lesson activities that support the journey through the steps of the Learning Challenge. In Part II of this book, you'll find the Lesson Ideas. For clarity and consistency, the Lesson Ideas have been presented so that each one follows the same format and structure, using headings and sub-headings that are common to every lesson. This structure clearly highlights where you are in relation to the four key steps of the Learning Challenge. This common format is designed to enable you to readily and confidently work with your students on a range of different Learning Challenge lesson ideas.

► Figure 1.2: **Lesson Structure Master**

| ACTIVITY TITLE:<br>*Craft an engaging title to 'hook' your learners.* | STRATEGIES USED:<br>*Choose 1-3 of the Learning Challenge strategies listed in Chapter 2 that you can use throughout your lesson.* |
|---|---|
| OVERVIEW:<br>*What key skills and concepts will your students learn in this lesson? What prior knowledge do they need to have?* | |
| KEY CONCEPT:<br>*What is the primary idea or concept that you want your students to understand?* | 1. IDENTIFY IMPORTANT CONCEPTS:<br>*What additional concepts are related to your key concepts? What other angles or avenues might your learners explore as they develop a deeper understanding of the key concept?* |
| KEY SKILLS:<br>*What are the primary skills that your students will use to arrive at a deeper understanding of the key concept?* | |
| KEY WORDS:<br>*What additional vocabulary words would aid learners in attaining a nuanced understanding of the concept?* | [OPTIONAL] ACTIVITY 1:<br>*Outline the first activity in your lesson, using one of the strategies you chose above. This activity should provoke discussion and elicit students' initial ideas about the key concept.* |
| LEARNING INTENTIONS: | |
| SUCCESS CRITERIA:<br>*We can . . .*<br>• <br>• <br>• <br>• | |

As you become more familiar and well-practised at using this structure, you may wish to develop your own ideas – or modify some of the Lesson Ideas we have provided. To enable you to do this, we have included a blank lesson structure master (like the one shown in Figure 1.2) for you to download. This is available on the companion website: http://resources.corwin.com/learningchallengelessons.

## 1.2 LEARNING INTENTIONS

The intended outcomes of the lesson ideas in this book are to help your students develop the following personal habits, abilities and attitudes:

1. An enquiring outlook coupled with an ability to articulate problems

2. A tendency to be intellectually proactive and persistent

3. A capacity for imaginative and adventurous thinking

4. A habit of exploring alternative possibilities

5. An ability to critically examine issues

6. A capacity for sound independent judgement

The lesson ideas also aim to help your students develop social habits and dispositions such as:

1.  Actively listening to others and trying to understand their viewpoints

2.  Giving reasons for what you say and expecting the same of others

3.  Exploring disagreements reasonably

4.  Being generally cooperative and constructive

5.  Being socially communicative and inclusive

6.  Taking other people's feelings and concerns into account

Each of these can be achieved through the type of high-quality dialogue that the lesson ideas in this book are intended to generate.

# 1.3 HIGH-QUALITY DIALOGUE

The lesson ideas in this book rely on the use of high-quality dialogue.

Dialogue is of high quality when it:

1.  challenges ideas, reasons and assumptions;

2.  makes participants **'wobble'**;

3.  leads to deeper thinking; and

4.  encourages participants to co-construct meaning together.

In the most basic sense, dialogue is the to and fro of talk between people who want to be understood. However, dialogue is not just 'conversation'. Whereas a conversation might go nowhere (or indeed anywhere), a dialogue properly defined and conducted always goes *somewhere* (for example, answering or examining a key question that was identified in the early stages of the dialogue).

Dialogue isn't just something that happens *between* people, it also takes place *within* people, in that thinking is rather like an inner dialogue. At least some forms of thinking are. Perhaps not the subconscious, automatic type of thinking, but certainly the reflective, ponderous form of thinking can be said to be an internal dialogue. This makes dialogue all the more important. If the patterns of talk established in communication with others influence our patterns of internal dialogue, then dialogue leads to thinking itself.

Dialogue is not the **Initiation–Response–Evaluation (IRE)** model of questioning that is used in many classrooms. IRE is a teacher-led, three-part sequence that begins with the teacher asking a student a question or introducing a topic for the purpose of finding out whether the student knows an answer. Although this style of questioning does have some place in education, it is only really a way of checking students' factual recall. It tends not to be very productive in terms of higher-order thinking, nor particularly useful for dialogue. Even if a higher-order question is posed, generally only one student gets to answer the question before the teacher evaluates the answer and ends any form of discussion.

Dialogue is not debate. Though many people use the term 'debate' when talking about dialogue, they are not one and the same thing. Debate is a type of classroom talk that, like IRE and conversation, has its purpose and benefits, but also its limitations. In debate, the situation is typically set up to create polarised views – usually a 'for' and 'against' group, with participants encouraged to express opinions that support only their side of the argument.

Debate encourages students to give reasons, to talk for an extended period, to participate and to use the language of persuasion. However, the main purpose of debate is to win the battle and persuade others to agree with a particular view. This means that students may not listen properly to opposing points of view and instead just present their own perspective. There might also be less value placed on co-constructing new understandings or preparing counter-arguments, and more emphasis on preparing winning statements or assertions.

Dialogue is about working collaboratively to understand what has not yet been understood and to form reasoned judgements and inferences. The IRE structure is compatible with dialogue, but it is not the same as dialogue. Dialogue can take participants further. It can help your students to become capable thinkers who are willing, able to learn and who can reason and express themselves clearly and confidently. At its best, dialogue will also foster encouragement, engagement, understanding and exploration.

Dialogue is a supremely flexible and stimulating instrument of thought. As children get older, the issues they need to understand, the judgements they need to make and the relationships they need to maintain become more complex. The turn-taking structure of dialogue that leads a child to learn the rudiments of language also serves as a means of thinking about complex issues. Thus, dialogue is holistic in its intentions and its outcomes.

Within high-quality dialogue, participants take actions (or make 'moves') that help to deepen thinking. In turn, this deeper thinking helps to develop an experiential understanding of the features listed in the concepts column of Figure 1.3.

▶ **Figure 1.3: Concepts and Actions in High-Quality Dialogue**

| Type of Thinking | Dialogue 'Moves' | Concepts |
|---|---|---|
| Productive | Generating ideas, generating alternative ideas, listing | Alternative, list, collection, class, category |
| Collaborative | Listening, taking turns, suspending judgement, establishing and applying 'ground rules' | Community |
| Creating Meaning | Questioning, classifying, comparing, ranking, connecting, clarifying, exemplifying, offering analogies, interpreting, summarising, defining, elaborating | Same, different, principle, example, important, significant, special, ordinary, function, purpose, part, whole, multiple, single, complete, incomplete, class, category, all, some, none, many |
| Argumentation (Argumentation to be used as the pursuit of truth rather than simply 'arguing' as children might argue over a toy. All reasons and ideas should be considered in this process.) | Agreeing, disagreeing, making an argument, questioning assumptions, assessing evidence | Opinion, belief, proposition, conclusion, claim, reason, premise, argument, cause, effect, symptom, consequence, true or false, agree, disagree, doubt, class, category, all, some, none, many, assumption, evidence, criteria, proof, judgement, justify |
| Speculative | Hypothesising, predicting, imagining, offering thought experiments | Cause, effect, symptom, consequence, theory, hypothesis |

# 1.4 EXPLORATORY TALK

One way to think about dialogue is as **exploratory talk**. Neil Mercer (2000) describes exploratory talk as:

> . . . that in which partners engage critically but constructively with each other's ideas. Relevant information is offered for joint consideration. Proposals may be challenged and counter-challenged but if so, reasons are given, and alternatives are offered. Agreement is sought as a basis for joint progress. Knowledge is made publicly accountable and reasoning is visible in the talk. (Mercer, 2000: 16)

However, when Rupert Wegerif (2002) looked into the types of talk found in classrooms, he discovered very little exploratory talk occurs when students work together in groups. Instead, the less learning-focused types of talk predominate, with students leaning more towards **disputational** or **cumulative talk**.

Cumulative talk is characterised by repetitions, confirmations and elaborations. It is typically heard when friendship groups work together or when an unfamiliar group is getting to know each other. The talk is positive and affirming, making everyone feel included and welcome. The participants rarely criticise each other or the ideas being put forward. Not everyone in the group takes part, nor are they expected to. The group accepts first ideas and does not try to go beyond these. This leads to an accumulation of 'common knowledge' and a sense of 'harmony in the group'.

Cumulative talk might not seem such a bad thing because it tends to be friendly and collaborative. However, rarely does cumulative talk involve challenge or rethinking beyond the first idea. Very little critical or creative thinking is evident. Reasons tend to be vague and are generally intended to affirm rather than examine.

The opposite of cumulative talk is disputational talk. This type of talk is less prevalent and is actually quite hard to spot because it can occur 'under the radar'. It is much more negative than cumulative talk. Disputational talk is critical of individuals (and their ideas), focuses on differences, is competitive and is all about being seen to 'win'. Groups engaged in disputational talk do not work together, nor pool their resources/intellect. Individuals within the group dominate. Mistakes are criticised and perhaps even ridiculed.

To ensure that the lesson ideas in this book work as well as intended, it is important that you encourage (and teach) your students to use exploratory talk. Exploratory talk is characterised by longer exchanges, use of questions, **reflection**, explanation and speculation. It should make full use of critical thinking and should also be very creative.

To engage in exploratory talk, your students should explore ideas and offer reasons for their thinking; they should also expect to be challenged by other students. Any challenges they make should be accompanied by reasons so that the whole group can learn from the interaction. There should be no risk of losing face if they get it 'wrong' because all statements should be offered in the expectation of helping everyone to make progress. The connection between this type of talk and improved language **skills**, both in general and in subject specific terms, should become apparent as your students process the information at their own level and then seek to go beyond it.

Exploratory talk occurs in an environment in which students feel comfortable to explore ideas with, and to trust in, each other. This means your students will need to recognise the benefits of collaborative learning and to know that when viewpoints are expressed, challenged or explored, it is always for the purpose of gaining new understanding and not for point-scoring or the belittling of others.

Making this a reality in the classroom requires some careful planning and preparation. An explicit set of ground-rules can help to provide the structure needed for exploratory talk to flourish. These could be as follows:

- We share our ideas and listen to each other.
- We talk one at a time.
- We respect each other's opinions.
- We give reasons to explain our ideas.
- If we disagree, we ask 'why?'
- We try to agree in the end if we can.

These rules are not set in stone! You do not have to use these rules. Indeed, it might be better to create a set of rules with your students. That way, they will have a sense of ownership and will be more likely to understand the meanings fully.

Whichever way you decide to go – presenting the list above or creating a new list with your students – you should ensure there is an opportunity for your students to talk about the meanings of the rules and to agree the precise wording of the rules.

Once this is complete, make sure the ground rules are displayed prominently for ease of reference and as a reminder. This might seem unnecessary. Yet, researchers have found that where there are a simple set of agreed ground rules that are constantly referred to, this has a far greater influence on improving the quality and focus of dialogues than if the rules are established and not frequently referred to. This is particularly true when students are working in smaller collaborative groups.

# 1.5 UNDERPINNING VALUES

There are many values and beliefs upon which the Learning Challenge lessons are based. Here are the most important ones.

### Challenge Makes Learning More Interesting

At the heart of the Learning Challenge is the belief that challenge makes learning more stimulating and worthwhile. This is in contrast to making learning simpler and more elementary, which has its place but is not ideal much of the time.

To illustrate the point, please compare the two paths shown in Figure 1.4. As you will see, the path on the left is straightforward and is likely to get you to your destination quickly, whereas the path to the right is filled with obstacles and will require greater effort to reach your goal. Of course, if you were in a rush, then the obvious path to take is the one on the left.

But if we were to ask you to choose the path most *interesting,* then which one would you go for? Which one looks to be the more engaging and thought-provoking? Which one is

► Figure 1.4: **The Path to Challenge**

most likely to lead you into discussion with other people about the best strategies going forward? Which one are you most likely to look back on and review with enthusiasm? Which is going to give you the most satisfaction when you eventually reach your goal? And which route are you most likely to remember months, maybe even years from now because of the effort you had to put in to get through it?

Hopefully, you've answered 'the right path' to each of those questions. If not, then we've got a persuasion job on our hands as well as an instructional one!

All of the lesson ideas in this book are designed to encourage participants to take the more challenging 'path' so that they think more, engage with ideas and each other more, and develop strategies for making sense of the problems they are faced with.

## We Are All Fallible

The Learning Challenge lessons encourage *all* participants, including the teacher or facilitator, to be open about their own fallibility and to willingly explore flaws in their own thinking so that everyone may learn more together. This means that phrases such as 'I'm not sure', 'perhaps', 'maybe' and 'I was wondering' are to be encouraged throughout the lessons. To some people, these sorts of phrases reveal ignorance or weak-mindedness. Yet in the context of the Learning Challenge, they are intended to reveal the ideals of open-mindedness and hypothesis-testing.

As Bertrand Russell wrote in an essay lamenting the rise of Nazism in 1933, 'The fundamental cause of the trouble is that in the modern world the stupid are cock-sure whilst the intelligent are full of doubt'. Or, as the celebrated Irish poet W.B. Yeats wrote in 'The Second Coming', 'The best lack all conviction, while the worst are full of passionate intensity' (Yeats, 1996 [1919]).

When your students engage with the Learning Challenge lessons, remind them of the benefits of being open-minded and explorative.

Linked to these ideals is the notion that there might not be one, agreed 'right' answer at the end of it all. Although most of the time some form of agreement is attainable, there are occasions, particularly with the more open-ended, philosophical questions, when no satisfactory conclusion is achievable in the timeframe you have. But that is not to say the experience will be any less worthwhile. It is to say that process is just as important as product, as explored in the next value below.

## Process Is As Important As Outcome

The process of learning is often more important than getting the right answer, particularly with Learning Challenge lessons. A learning focus includes an emphasis on questioning, challenging, striving to get better and on beating personal bests. This contrasts with a performance focus that hinges on grades, attainment, showing what you can do and on beating each other.

As numerous teachers and their students will testify, far too many schools focus primarily on performance ('it's the grades that count'). And yet improved performance comes from a learning focus, whereas learning does *not* always come from a performance focus.

If you and your students focus on *learning,* then their performance grades will also increase. However, if you and your students focus on grades alone, then rich learning opportunities might be missed along the way.

That is why *process* is more important than getting the answer right in Learning Challenge lessons. Of course, if you can get your students to deeply engage in learning *and* help them to reach a satisfactory answer, then that is ideal. But if your students go into the pit and don't come out (yet), then don't worry: it doesn't mean they haven't benefited from the experience, so long as you keep encouraging them to go beyond their first answers.

You want your students to seek alternative explanations, to ask questions such as *why, if* and *what about*, and to see problems as part of the learning process rather than things to be avoided. Encouraging students to make connections, find the significance of parts in relation to the whole and look for ways to transfer ideas to other contexts will *improve* their competence rather than them simply *proving* they have got the right answer.

# CHAPTER 2

# The Lesson Activities

## 2.0 OVERVIEW

The lesson activities in this book are all designed around the Learning Challenge. They make use of dialogue strategies such as Mysteries, Ranking, Opinion Lines and Venn Diagrams. This chapter gives a very brief overview of some of the approaches. For a much more in-depth guide to the Learning Challenge, we recommend *The Learning Challenge* by James Nottingham (2017). For a deeper insight into the other strategies, then we recommend *Challenging Learning Through Dialogue* by Nottingham, Nottingham and Renton (2017).

## 2.1 MYSTERIES

To help get your students into the pit – and then out again – we have recommended many techniques. Mysteries are perhaps our favourite.

A Mystery is a problem-solving activity based around a central question that is open to more than one reasonable answer.

The information or 'clues' needed to answer the question are presented on separate slips of paper so that your students can analyse, sort, sequence and link them together.

The questions at the heart of Mysteries tend to be matters of interpretation, judgement and argument. They often involve dialogues on causation or speculation about consequences.

Characteristics of a Mystery include the following:

1. They begin with a key question or dilemma that should create cognitive conflict in the minds of your students.
2. They generally revolve around a central character.
3. Some clues include ambiguous information.
4. Some clues include irrelevant or contradictory information.
5. Some clues are pure 'red herrings' designed to deter easy answers.
6. Some clues can't be fully understood in the absence of other clues.
7. The subject matter ought to be relevant and of interest to participants.

### Set Up

Print a set of clues for each group. You will need to split your students into small groups (a maximum of four students per group). Each group will need their own set of clues.

Depending on the particular Mystery, the clues will either come in a first, second and third batch or just in one big batch. This will be made clear at the beginning of each of the lesson ideas.

## Exploration Phase

Ask each group to lay all the clues you have given them out on the table in front of them. Once they have read through each one, get them to group, connect or in some way sort the clues. This 'movement' is a crucial feature of the task, contributing in large measure to its effectiveness as a classroom strategy for thinking.

Remind all your students as follows:

1. This is a group activity and so everyone in the group should be taking an active role.

2. They should choose categories for their clues. This might range from relevant/ irrelevant to personal/background, or fact/opinion, supporting/contradictory, etc. Do not impose these categories – let your students come up with their own categories as this is an important part of the learning process.

3. Mysteries are all about dialogue. So, there should be lots of talk, including explanation, reasoning, counter-examples, challenges and questioning.

4. When moving slips of paper around, your students should always give each other an explanation why. They should not let anyone take over and do all the sorting and classifying without seeking the opinions and responses of others.

5. The task is an open one and may have quite a few possible 'right' answers. If they are doing it correctly, then they may often change their minds when they see fresh connections or spot logical patterns they hadn't noticed before.

## Comparison of Strategy

After your students have had enough time in their groups to process and begin categorising the clues, ask each group to explain their strategy to the whole class. This should throw up some differences in approach and therefore provide cause for reflection.

## Main Activity

After your students have had the chance to hear what strategies and categories other groups are using, they should begin to move more definitely towards answering the key question (for example, 'Who was responsible for the death of William in Mary Shelley's *Frankenstein*?' Lesson Idea 1 in this book). As they do this, remind them to make good use of these thinking and dialogue skills:

| | |
|---|---|
| • Sorting relevant information | • Checking and refining |
| • Interpreting information | • Explaining, reasoning and justifying |
| • Using inference and deduction skills | • Problem solving |
| • Making links between the clues | • Decision making |
| • Speculating to form hypotheses | |

As you circulate around the groups, use some of the following terms:

| | | | | |
|---|---|---|---|---|
| enquire | infer | plan | link/connect | refine |
| probable | analyse | hypothesise | conclude | data |
| evidence | possible | sequence | predict | certain |

So, for example, you might say some of the following things to particular groups:

- Which pieces of information have you linked or connected?
- Which of those pieces are more probable than others?
- What is your hypothesis in terms of the sequence of events?
- What do you infer from this piece of data?

You will know when the main activity phase is drawing to a close when each group begins to draw some conclusions. The best situation will be that your students offer their conclusions with an air of open-mindedness, in the knowledge that their conclusions aren't quite definite. If, on the other hand, they seem very sure about their ideas, then you should try to create at least some uncertainty through questioning and drawing their attention to conflicting pieces of evidence.

## Presentations and Reflection

Ask each group to present their findings to the whole class. To ensure that all students get a fair chance to speak (rather than just the more dominant characters), you might like to use the Talking Heads method of selection as described in *Challenging Learning Through Dialogue* (Nottingham, Nottingham and Renton, 2017: Section 7.5).

As each group presents their conclusions, encourage all the other groups to identify similarities and differences when compared with their own findings.

The differences might be to do with content, for example, the students might say, 'We decided that Romeo is not necessarily in love because the evidence only points to how he is struck by Juliet's beautiful appearance'. (See Lesson Plan 11 in this book.)

Or it might be to do with process, for example, 'We divided our clues into relevant, irrelevant and could be relevant; whereas the group presenting their findings split their clues into personal, background and red herrings'.

After each group has presented their conclusions, use some of the following metacognitive questions to review the learning journey:

1. What information helped you?
2. Which clues were misleading?
3. How did you categorise the clues? If you were to do this again, what categories would you go for next time?
4. What role did you play within your group? In what way would you act or think differently next time?
5. What degree of certainty do you have about your group's conclusion?
6. Is uncertainty a good thing? How does it make you feel? What are its benefits?

For more information about how to run a Mystery – and about how to write your own – go to Chapter 8 in *Challenging Learning Through Dialogue* (Nottingham, Nottingham and Renton, 2017).

# 2.2 RANKING

A useful way for your students to sort out all their ideas is through ranking. This can be done in a Linear Rank, a Diamond Rank, a Pyramid Rank or any such shape that will prompt your students to analyse the relative value of each answer. Each time we have suggested ranking in the lesson ideas, we have given our recommendation as to the style to go for. Do not feel obliged to stick to this type of ranking; if another shape seems more appropriate, then encourage your students to go for that instead.

Please note that some students will simply 'rank' characteristics in alphabetical order, particularly when they are finding the idea of ranking too challenging. If your students do this, then gently remind them that the task is not to 'sort' but to 'rank' and that alphabetical order is not a rank. If alphabetical order was indeed a rank, then words beginning with 'a' would be seen as more valuable than words beginning with b, c or d!

## Diamond Ranking

The Diamond Ranking strategy encourages active participation. It will help your students prioritise information, clarify their thoughts and create reasons and reflections.

Your students must place the statement with the highest priority at the top of the formation and the least important statement at the bottom. The second, third and fourth rows consist of statements that are ranked with descending priority, with each row having two, three and two statements respectively.

Diamond Ranking looks like the illustration shown in Figure 2.1.

▶ **Figure 2.1: Diamond Ranking**

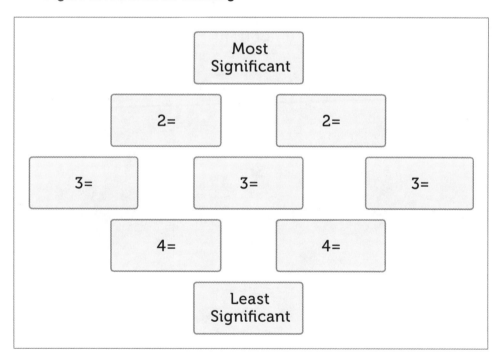

## Pyramid Ranking

Pyramid Ranking is similar to Diamond Ranking except that it is in the shape of a pyramid or triangle. This allows different numbers of factors to be ranked compared to Diamond Ranking. Figure 2.2 shows a Pyramid Rank.

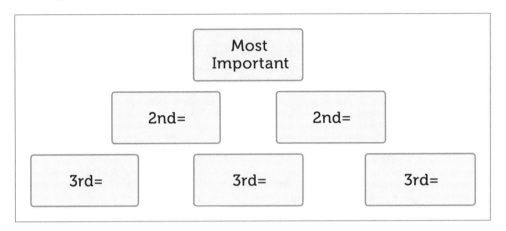

## Linear Ranking

Linear Ranking often leads to more deliberation than the other two styles of ranking because there are no 'equal' spots. Instead, each characteristic should be given a position that is different from any other. However, as with all the other ranks, this position can be decided on importance, relevance, significance or any other agreed quality.

▶ Figure 2.3: Linear Ranking

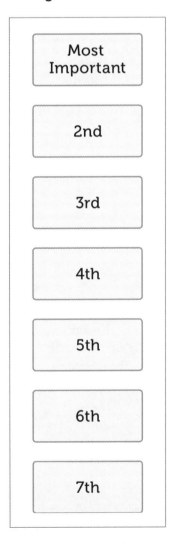

For more information about how to use ranking to help your students through the Learning Pit, go to Section 6.3.3 in *The Learning Challenge* by James Nottingham (2017).

## 2.3 SORTING AND CLASSIFYING WITH VENN DIAGRAMS

Sorting and Classifying are everyday, often unconscious skills that we use to organise information and ideas.

These are basic cognitive skills needed by all human beings to recognise similarities and differences through seeing common features, developing awareness of concepts and making links between them. Sorting and Classifying helps students to make sense of the world around them.

Venn Diagrams are great visual tools for thinking and effectively support the process of Sorting and Classifying. They even work with the youngest students so long as you separate out the overlapping category into a third circle. This is shown in Figure 2.4.

▶ **Figure 2.4: Using Venn Diagrams With Young Children**

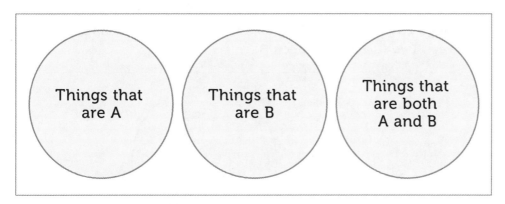

Of course, the normal way to draw a Venn Diagram is as shown in Figure 2.5 with the overlapping circles.

▶ **Figure 2.5: Using Venn Diagrams With Older Students**

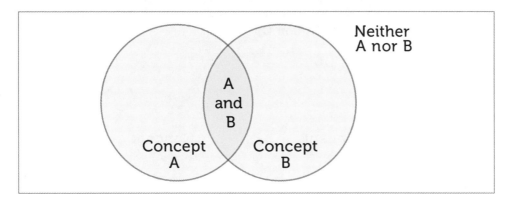

Sometimes during a Learning Challenge lesson, your students will find it useful to examine the relationship between two or more connected concepts. Venn Diagrams can help with this. For example, you could ask them to decide which of the following variations best represent the relationship:

▶ **Figure 2.6: Using Venn Diagrams to Identify the Relationship Between Two Concepts (Option A)**

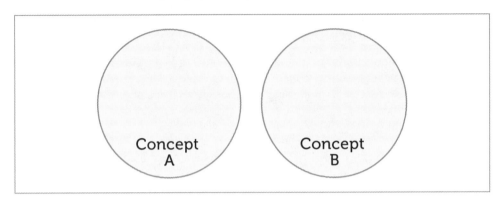

Option A: Both concepts are distinct from each other

▶ **Figure 2.7: Using Venn Diagrams to Identify the Relationship Between Two Concepts (Option B)**

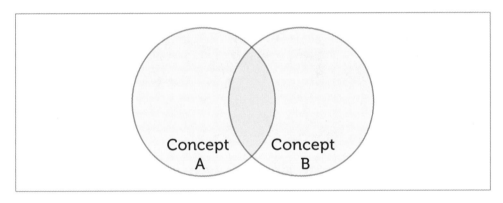

Option B: Both concepts are overlapping but not the same as each other

▶ **Figure 2.8: Using Venn Diagrams to Identify the Relationship Between Two Concepts (Option C)**

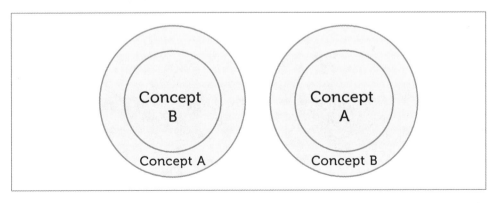

Option C: One concept is always a version of the other

For more information about how to use Venn Diagrams to help your students through the pit, go to Section 6.3.9 in *The Learning Challenge* by James Nottingham (2017).

## 2.4 OPINION LINES

Opinion Lines are very useful for beginning to explore statements using examples, gauging degrees of agreement and disagreement, or identifying degrees of preference.

### Setting up an Opinion Line

1. Create a line long enough for all your students to stand along. If you can mark this with a rope or some string, then that might help.

2. Mark one end with a 'Completely Agree' sign and the other with a 'Completely Disagree' sign. Talk through the other descriptors shown in this diagram if you think it will help your students to understand the degrees of agreement and disagreement:

▶ **Figure 2.9: Opinion Line Diagram**

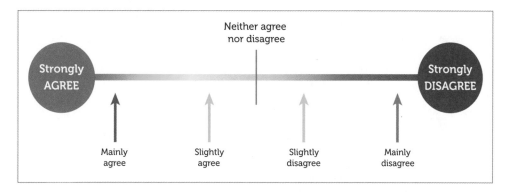

3. Explain to your students that you are going to give them a statement to think about (we have given recommendations within the lesson ideas). Say they will have time to think about it first, then you will ask them to stand on the part of the line that corresponds with how much they agree or disagree with the statement.

4. Once your students have taken a place on the line, get them to talk with the people around them to compare their reasons for standing where they are. The following prompts should help them to ensure their conversation is more exploratory (see Section 1.4) than cumulative:

   • What do you think?

   • What are your reasons?

   • I agree with you because . . .

   • I disagree with you because . . .

   • Is there another way of looking at this?

   • What if . . . ?

   • Have we considered all the factors?

   • What have we agreed?

Please note that Opinion Lines do not have to go from 'completely agree' to 'completely disagree'. They could range from fact to opinion; probably true to definitely true; or reasonable opinion to unreasonable opinion, for example. Also, the lines don't have to be physical lines; they can be drawn on paper, with your students pointing to the part of the line that they would stand at if the line were big enough to do so.

For more information about Opinion Lines, go to Section 7.2 in *Challenging Learning Through Dialogue* by Nottingham, Nottingham and Renton (2017).

## 2.5 OPINION CORNERS

Opinion Corners have a similar structure to Opinion Lines, so can be introduced in a similar way. The main difference is that using the corners will prevent your students from 'sitting on the fence' because they are required to choose from one of four descriptors: Strongly Agree; Agree; Disagree; Strongly Disagree. Set up Opinion Corners as shown in Figure 2.10.

▶ **Figure 2.10: Opinion Corners**

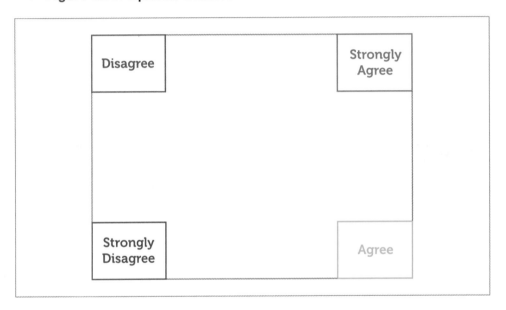

After you read a statement (examples can be found in *Challenging Learning Through Dialogue* and within the lesson activities in this book), your students should stand in the corner that best represents their opinion on the matter. Tell them they have to choose one of the corners. They cannot stand somewhere in the middle. They must make a decision as to the one that is the best description of their opinion. They are allowed to move if they change their minds, but even then they should move from one corner to another rather than to the middle or off to a side somewhere.

Once your students have chosen a corner, get them to talk about their choice with the people around them. After that, get a spokesperson from each corner to give a summary of the reasons why the people in 'their' corner made the choice they did. This will give your students the chance to hear different perspectives on the issue.

In comparison to Opinion Lines, Opinion Corners emphasise the different views everyone holds, and introduce quite distinct groupings. For that reason, Opinion Corners are very useful in developing not only skills of reasoning and explanation, but also the language of persuasion.

For more information about Opinion Corners, go to Section 7.3 in *Challenging Learning Through Dialogue* by Nottingham, Nottingham and Renton (2017).

## 2.6 FORTUNE LINES

Similar to the 'Mystery' strategy in Section 2.1, a Fortune Line gives students evidence to evaluate and analyse. As with the Mystery, the activity challenges students to make decisions about the importance and relevance of the information before them and apply reasoning to the conclusions they draw. How your students link together the information and what they infer from it will provide an ideal way to get into and out of the pit.

Unlike a Mystery, however, a Fortune Line requires students to interpret a chain of events *and* link them to a wider range of variables represented by the axes of a graph. In this way, the focus of Fortune Line activities is to explore two aspects of the information at the same time. This is typically emotions, fortunes or experiences on one axis and time or chronology on the other.

Like any normal graph, Fortune Lines are open to interpretation: they give a 'big picture', from which the reader can draw conclusions. The main difference though between Fortune Lines and 'normal' graphs is that Fortune Line axes are left deliberately vague so as to add further challenge to the idea of interpreting events.

For example, rather than listing the months of the year on the x-axis as with a normal graph, a Fortune Line might instead just say 'Time'. This means that the Fortune Line could be representing a week, a year, a decade or a century – or indeed any length of time: it is for the students to decide as they interpret the story.

Each Fortune Line will have a set of key events printed onto card. Your students should take each 'event' in turn and place them on the graph in the place that they think is most appropriate. The line on this graph will have already been plotted before it is given to the students. This will then help your students to create a narrative about the main character or experiences. Note that, as with Mysteries, Fortune Lines will always have ambiguous or purposefully misleading information included in among the event cards. This is to encourage more thinking, questioning and deliberation.

▶ **Figure 2.11: Fortune Line**

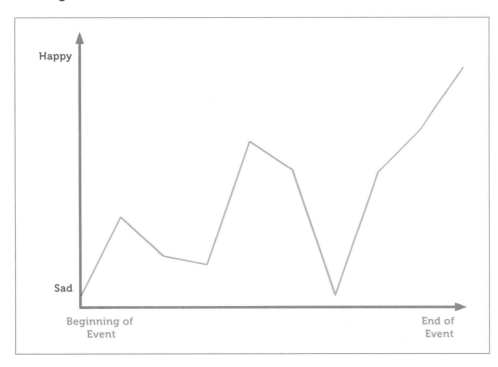

### Using Fortune Lines

Divide your students into small groups. Give them the Fortune Line first, then give them the associated set of statements.

Ask them to do the following:

- Analyse the pattern of information presented by the graph.
- Decide which of the statements or scenarios helps to explain the pattern of information on the graph and indicate which part of the graph it helps to explain.
- Place the statements on the graph to show where they think they best fit.
- Develop a narrative of events that explains the graph.

Please note that in some circumstances, your students should be presented with a blank Fortune Line and then asked to create the line(s) as they interpret the information.

For more information about Fortune Lines, go to Chapter 10 in *Challenging Learning Through Dialogue* by Nottingham, Nottingham and Renton (2017).

## 2.7 LIVING GRAPHS

This is very much a variation of a Fortune Line. A line graph is plotted by the students with key events or actions as markers. These key events or actions are provided on cards.

Like the Fortune Line, a Living Graph usually has time represented across the x-axis. Students must take account of both when the events occur and their significance (the y-axis). This significance can be in terms of things, such as well-being, usefulness, difficulty, energy used, emotional cost, etc.

▶ **Figure 2.12: Living Graph**

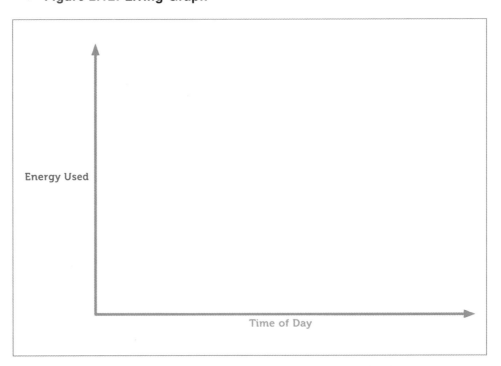

Setting the Scene

# 2.8 CONCEPT LINES

Concept Lines have a similar structure to Opinion Lines so can be introduced in a similar way. The main difference is that the line now represents characteristics of a concept rather than degrees of agreement or disagreement.

Encourage your students to list all the terms and ideas that they have used in connection with the central concept. Then get them to place the terms along the line, being careful to place them in order of meaning or significance. The example in Figure 2.13 should help to illustrate the technique.

▶ **Figure 2.13: Concept Line Example – Friendliness**

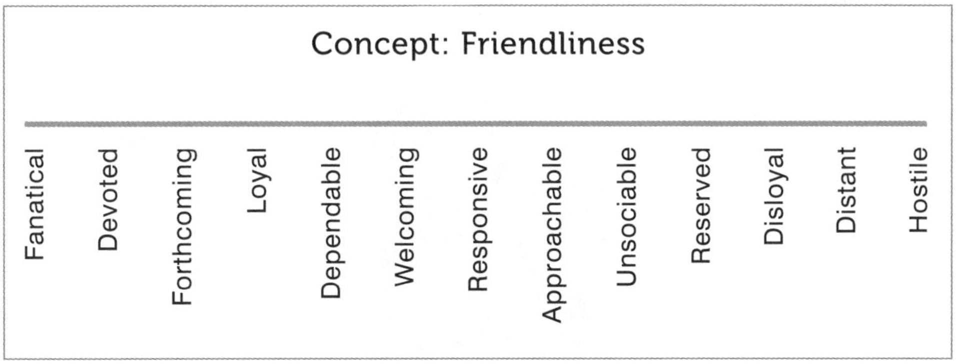

Concept: Friendliness

Fanatical | Devoted | Forthcoming | Loyal | Dependable | Welcoming | Responsive | Approachable | Unsociable | Reserved | Disloyal | Distant | Hostile

For more information about Concept Lines, go to Section 6.3.6 in *The Learning Challenge* by James Nottingham (2017).

# 2.9 ODD ONE OUT

Students are presented with a group of objects, numbers, mathematical problems, words, text passages, poems, shapes, scientific elements, geographical concepts, etc., to be compared and contrasted. They are then asked to identify the odd one out. This apparently simple question encourages students to explore and focus on the characteristics of the items in question and fosters an understanding of relationships between them. There should be a large number of possible correct answers that students can provide, and students should always be encouraged to give a fully explained and justified answer. The lesson ideas in this book use groups of three images and this is the recommended number for making Odd One Out work successfully.

It is an inclusive activity because you can accept any of the three options as the correct answer (as long as your students' reasoning is consistent and sound). Asking students to make *each* item or image the odd one out will encourage your students to go beyond their first idea and to explore further possibilities. This can serve to deepen their thinking. Collecting and recording your students' thinking on a whiteboard or flipchart is a good idea because this demonstrates the inclusive nature of the task. The shared vocabulary that emerges gives students an ownership of the task, which hopefully serves to engage and motivate them.

When you first show the three Odd One Out items, you should give your students a short time to think to themselves (Think). Then you can give them 30 seconds or so for paired dialogue (Pair). This will give them the opportunity to explore additional responses, ask each other questions, view things from a different perspective and practise the vocabulary they need to answer the question. Finally, you can ask your students to share their ideas with the whole group (Share).

▶ **Figure 2.14: Odd One Out**

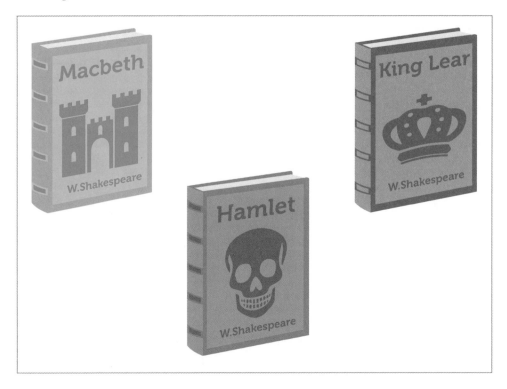

For more information about Odd One Out, go to section 9 in *Challenging Learning Through Dialogue* (Nottingham, Nottingham and Renton, 2017).

## 2.10 CONCEPT TARGET

Concept Targets are a highly effective tool to use with students. Your students can use a Concept Target to clarify the criteria and characteristics of a concept.

To use a Concept Target, your students should draw an inner and outer circle as shown in Figure 2.15 below. In the inner circle they should write the key concept and in the outer circle they should write all the ideas that relate to that concept or that have emerged through the dialogue process.

Students should take each idea in turn and decide whether it is a necessary characteristic of the concept (in which case they should move it to the inner circle), a probable characteristic (in which case they should leave it in the outer circle) or a very rare characteristic (in which case they should move it outside of the outer circle).

Your students might like to use relative positions to describe the degree to which each particular idea is a characteristic of the concept.

For more information about Concept Targets, go to Section 6.3 in *The Learning Challenge* by James Nottingham (2017).

► **Figure 2.15: Concept Target**

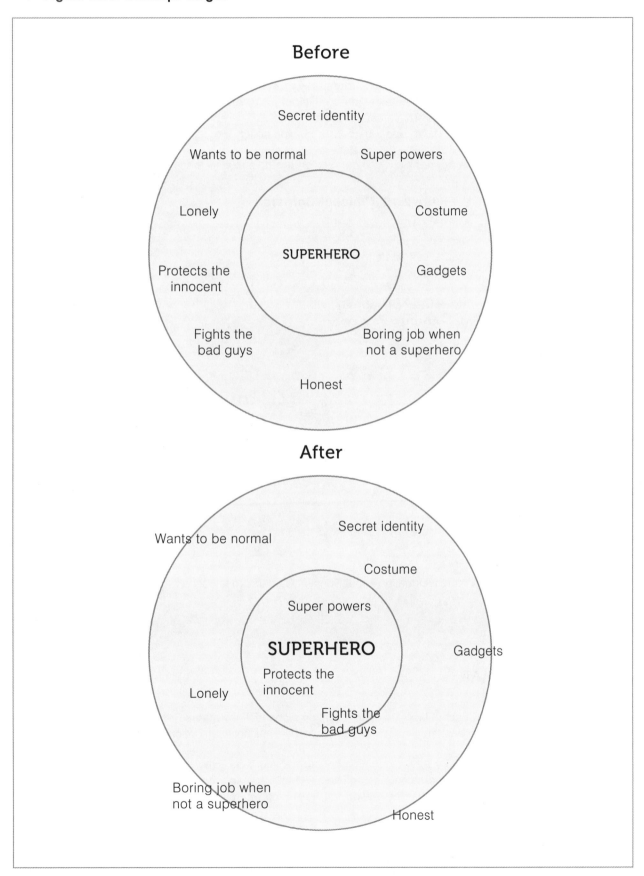

**Before**

Secret identity

Wants to be normal          Super powers

Lonely                    Costume

**SUPERHERO**

Protects the                 Gadgets
innocent

Fights the            Boring job when
bad guys            not a superhero

Honest

**After**

Wants to be normal          Secret identity

Costume

Super powers

**SUPERHERO**

Protects the                          Gadgets
innocent

Lonely

Fights the
bad guys

Boring job when
not a superhero

Honest

# 2.11 CONCEPT CORNERS

Concept Corners are derived from the Concept Table tool shown in section 6.3.8 of *The Learning Challenge* book by James Nottingham (2017).

When using Concept Corners, ask your students to write the key concept in the middle of the table, then ask them to think of examples for each of the categories selected for the corners. These categories are: 'phrases', 'examples', 'synonyms and antonyms' and 'related ideas' (see Figure 2.16) but you could use your own headings.

In the figure below, you can see an example related to the concept of 'colour'.

▶ **Figure 2.16: Concept Corners**

| Examples of phrases or sentences where the concept is used: | | Examples or contexts where concept applies: |
|---|---|---|
| The colour of money<br>Rose-coloured view | | Rainbows<br>Fruit<br>Art |
| | **Colour** | |
| Examples of wording phrases of similar or opposite meaning: | | Examples of related ideas or associations: |
| Shade<br>Tone | | Science<br>Art<br>Perception |

For more information about Concept Corners, go to Section 10.1, Figure 62, in *The Learning Challenge* by James Nottingham (2017).

# 2.12 CONCEPT MAP

A Concept Map (sometimes called a connections map) is a tool that enables students to demonstrate their understanding of the links between concepts or ideas within a concept.

As Figure 2.17 (below) demonstrates, students write the various relevant concepts or ideas in boxes and then make the links between them using lines. The key aspect of this strategy is that the *reason* for the link between the ideas or concepts is written on that joining line.

Knowing any number of key words or concepts is arguably surface level *knowledge*; making and describing the links between these words/concepts is a visual representation of a deeper *understanding*.

► Figure 2.17: **Concept Map**

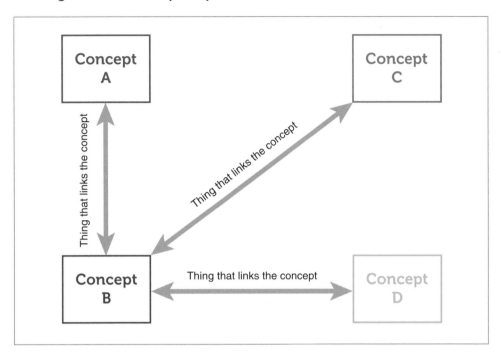

## 2.13 JIGSAW GROUPS

Jigsaw Grouping is a good way to maximise participation in dialogue. Assigning each student a 'jigsaw' piece of information will ensure that all of your students are dependent upon each other in order for everyone to succeed.

Where Jigsaw Groups have been used within the lessons in this book, the facilitation of this has been described in detail. You can find more on this approach in Section 7.6 of *Challenging Learning Through Dialogue* (Nottingham, Nottingham and Renton, 2017) or from the website Jigsaw Classroom (www.jigsaw.org).

# PART II: THE LESSON IDEAS

The lesson ideas are presented to you here, with each built around the same, consistent structure.

The resources for each lesson are available on the companion website: http://resources.corwin.com/learningchallengelessons. We recommend that for each lesson you print the associated activity cards and ask your students to help in cutting them.

After you have tried out a lesson with your students, you will find a page at the end of the lesson plan where you can reflect on the processes and learning that has occurred. It also allows you to think about how you would potentially do things differently if you taught the lesson again. These notes pages are titled WWW.EBI. You'll see that the page is split into two with WWW – **W**hat **W**orked **W**ell at the top and EBI – **E**ven **B**etter **I**f at the bottom.

# Who Was Responsible for the Death of William in Mary Shelley's *Frankenstein?*

**KEY CONCEPT:** Responsibility

**KEY SKILLS:** Crafting an argument

Citing textual evidence

Demonstrating understanding of figurative language and nuance

# Who Was Responsible for the Death of William in Mary Shelley's *Frankenstein?*

## OVERVIEW:

The lesson will enhance your students' knowledge and understanding of the novel *Frankenstein* by Mary Shelley, with focuses on characterisation, responsibility and developments in science. It is important for your students to be familiar with the novel prior to this activity.

## KEY CONCEPT:

Responsibility

## KEY WORDS:

Responsibility, duty, blame, crime, nature, science, morality, justice, obligation, loyalty, punishment, guilt, culpability, accountability, innocence, child, guardian, control, fear, family, deceit, revenge, pain, isolation and rejection.

## LEARNING INTENTION:

To understand how responsibility is embodied in the characters in the novel *Frankenstein*.

## SUCCESS CRITERIA:

We can do the following:

- Discuss and explore our understanding of responsibility.

- Examine the thoughts and behaviour of characters to discuss their role in the death of William.

- Determine the responsibility held by Victor Frankenstein and the creature.

- Reflect on and explain the significance of historical, cultural and societal context and its influence when deciding upon the allocation of responsibility.

## STRATEGIES USED:

Opinion Line

Mystery

# 1. IDENTIFY IMPORTANT CONCEPTS

Some of the key areas to investigate within and around the concept of 'responsibility' are the following:

- Guilt
- Morality
- Family
- Society
- Science
- Blame
- Regret
- Justice
- Equality

## Activity 1: Provoke the Discussion Using an Opinion Line

Encourage your students to think carefully about the statements on the **Activity 1 resource cards** (listed below) and discuss their ideas in pairs/groups.

- Parents have a responsibility to teach their child, but the child is responsible for their own actions.
- Children cannot be held responsible for their actions as they are still learning and growing.
- Rich people should have more responsibility than poor people.
- 'With great power comes great responsibility.' Voltaire
- 'The price of greatness is responsibility.' Winston Churchill
- 'You become responsible forever for what you've tamed.' Antoine de Saint-Exupery
- 'We are all members of one body. We are responsible for each other.' J.B. Priestley
- 'No snowflake in an avalanche ever feels responsible.' Stanislaw Jerzy Lec
- 'Winners take responsibility. Losers blame others.' Brit Hume
- 'An idea isn't responsible for the people who believe in it.' Don Marquis
- 'In dreams begin responsibility.' W.B. Yeats

**Download the activity cards at http://resources.corwin.com/ learningchallengelessons**

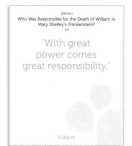

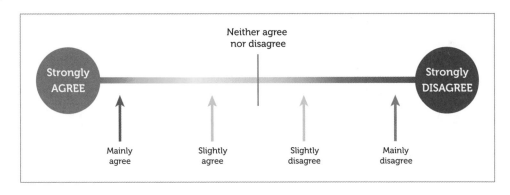

Who Was Responsible for the Death of William in Mary Shelley's *Frankenstein*?

**Challenging** LEARNING    35

After some consideration time, read out each quotation in turn, asking your students to position themselves on the line. The students should be encouraged to justify their place with reasons and there should be a whole group dialogue around each statement before moving on to another.

## 2. CHALLENGE STUDENTS' UNDERSTANDING OF THE CONCEPT

Here are some examples of cognitive conflict we expect your students to experience:

| Opinion | Conflicting Opinion |
|---|---|
| I am responsible for my own behaviour and the consequences of my behaviour. | My parents are responsible for me until I am 18 years old. |
| We are all responsible for our own actions. | Sometimes we act because we are following orders or instructions from others. |
| We must all be responsible for each other to help make the world a fairer place for everyone. | I can't be held responsible for the lives of others. I must focus on my own needs and the needs of my family. |
| Having responsibility makes me feel important. | Having responsibility makes me feel stressed. |
| Children cannot be trusted to be responsible. | When I was younger, I cared for and fed my guinea pigs every day to make sure they were healthy and happy. |
| Responsibility always falls to the eldest. | Everyone should take responsibility. |

### Questions for Challenge

- What is responsibility?
- How do we know what responsibility is?
- What makes someone responsible?
- Who decides if we are responsible or not?
- Is it possible for responsibility to be given to someone?
- How can responsibility be earned?
- Does being responsible always mean we are in control?
- How can we demonstrate responsibility?
- When is responsibility a choice?
- Is it irresponsible to refuse responsibility given to us?
- Can we stop being responsible for something or someone if we choose to?
- To what degree do we have to learn how to be responsible?
- Who decides what responsibility is?
- Should we always be held responsible for our actions?
- Can we ever be held responsible for something we didn't do?

- When might you be guilty of a crime but not be responsible?

- Should parents always be held responsible for the actions of their children?

- Are adults always more responsible than children?

- When is it irresponsible to take responsibility?

- What is the difference between taking responsibility and taking the blame?

- Should blame always fall on those who are responsible?

- When is responsibility the same as taking control of your actions?

- How responsible are we if someone else is controlling our actions?

- Can responsibility be taken away from you?

- Why did Winston Churchill say, 'The price of greatness is responsibility'?

- Why do some people have more responsibility?

- Should people with more knowledge and talent have more responsibility than others? Is this fair?

- Do you need to be human to be responsible?

- An experiment is a scientific procedure undertaken to make a discovery. Can we hold scientists responsible if these experiments go wrong?

# 3. CONSTRUCT UNDERSTANDING

Download the activity cards at
http://resources.corwin.com/
learningchallengelessons

### Activity 2: Mystery

In groups of 3 or 4, students are presented with the **Activity 2 resource cards** and are encouraged to use the information on the cards to answer the following key question:

**Who was responsible for the death of William?**

Encourage your students to explore what the language/devices reveal about the author's view.

It is often useful to support your students when they are sorting through the information in front of them. This can help them to interpret and handle the information more easily and reconstruct their thinking to reach an understanding. In the table below, students can record their ideas on who they believe is responsible for the death of William.

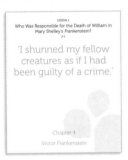

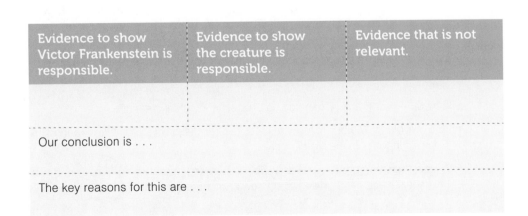

| Evidence to show Victor Frankenstein is responsible. | Evidence to show the creature is responsible. | Evidence that is not relevant. |
| --- | --- | --- |
| | | |

Our conclusion is . . .

The key reasons for this are . . .

## Questions to Promote Further Dialogue

- Who was responsible for William?

- Who was responsible for the creature?

- Can we be responsible for something we cannot control?

- Can we judge the creature by the same rules as we judge humans?

- Does the creature understand the concept of 'responsibility'?

- Do you need to understand the concept of 'responsibility' to be held responsible for your actions?

- How did the creature learn about rules and morality in society?

- If the creature is a scientific experiment, can it be held responsible for its own actions?

- Does the creature's appearance affect our view of its responsibility?

- If we create something, are we always responsible for it?

- Should Victor Frankenstein be held responsible for the creation and behaviour of the creature?

- Was Victor Frankenstein legally and/or morally responsible for the creature? How do you know this?

- Who made Victor Frankenstein responsible for the creature?

- Did Victor Frankenstein choose to take responsibility for the creature?

- Can you be wholly responsible for the actions of another?

- Was Victor Frankenstein irresponsible rather than responsible for the death of his brother?

- If we blame Victor Frankenstein for the actions of the creature, is this the same as saying he is responsible?

- Can you be held responsible for something you are afraid of?

- To what degree is society's rejection of the creature responsible for the events that followed?

- What is your interpretation of Mary Shelley's views on responsibility?

- At the end of the text, the creature states, 'Polluted by crimes and torn by the bitterest remorse, where can I find rest but in death?' What does this reveal about the creature's feelings of responsibility?

- Does the creature's regret suggest his responsibility?

- Did Victor Frankenstein know that the creature would kill William? Does this matter?

- Did the creature plan to kill William?

- Has Victor Frankenstein influenced the morals and behaviour of the creature?

- Who was responsible for the death of Justine?

- Why did Victor Frankenstein conduct his experiments in secret?

- Can we blame Victor Frankenstein for the results of his scientific experiment? Could he have predicted later events?

- In the 19th century, scientists were challenging and testing the boundaries between life and death, discovering new and improved methods of diagnosis and

treatments. Can scientists be wholly responsible for the consequences of their experiments?

- In a court of law, would the creature have been found guilty/responsible for the murder of William?

- Can Victor be responsible for and be a victim of the same crime?

- Are we shocked by the actions of the creature when it kills William?

- Does Mary Shelley present the creature as dangerous?

- Victor Frankenstein never gave his creation a name; does this change our view of its culpability?

- Did Victor Frankenstein have a moral and social responsibility to inform people about his creation? Would this have kept William alive?

- Did Victor Frankenstein have a responsibility to the world of science to experiment and advance the knowledge of man?

- Are there any sections in the novel where Victor Frankenstein does behave responsibly? Does this matter?

- If Felix had shown compassion and care towards the creature, would this have prevented the murder of William?

- Could responsibility for William's death lie elsewhere?

## Adaptation

You could select a smaller range of cards for your students to consider in the Mystery activity or offer them more adult support.

## Extension

Ask students to find their own evidence to determine who is responsible for the death of William.

Ask your students to consider how science may be responsible for the death of William. They could conduct detailed research into the developments of science during this time, and the unrestricted and illegal practices in medical research. Your students could structure their findings using a Thought Map. Once your students have conducted their research, ask them to search for evidence in the novel that would help them ascertain if science was responsible for the death of William. A Venn Diagram could be used to sort and classify their ideas and research.

Mary Shelley uses the subtitle 'The Modern Prometheus' for Frankenstein. Your students could discuss and explore the meanings and motivation behind this subtitle.

Challenge students to create a Fortune Line with the x-axis being time and the y-axis 'level of responsibility' (zero responsibility to absolute responsibility). Ask your students to look through the cards from the Mystery activity and position these on the graph, annotating the graph with their ideas at each stage.

Transform the Mystery activity into a drama performance of the trial for William's murder. Students could use the Mystery cards as evidence *for* and *against* the prosecution of the creature/Victor Frankenstein. Challenge the students to find more evidence from the book and from other areas such as religion and the developments in science during this period. This activity could be used to create a newspaper article and/or an essay.

# 4. CONSIDER THE LEARNING JOURNEY

At the end of the activity it is usual to encourage your students to review their learning journey and the thinking process they have engaged in throughout the session.

This can include reflection on the thinking that has taken place to this point, and a summary and conclusion of the new understanding reached.

Explicit reference to Learning Intentions and Success Criteria is a good starting point for this reflection.

To encourage the students to review their learning journey and their thinking progress, students should provide an argument and reasoning in response to the key question:

**Who was responsible for the death of William?**

In pairs/groups, students decide on who they believe is responsible for the death of William. They must provide three key reasons using evidence from the text.

Activities from the extension section could be useful for this stage such as the newspaper front page and/or the criminal trial for Victor Frankenstein/creature. The students could act as jurors and decide who they would convict, resulting in a short speech to the class. If your students have identified other agents who should be held responsible, then adapt the activity accordingly.

Possible questions to review the learning journey are as follows:

- Has anyone changed their mind about what it means to be responsible or to have responsibility?
- What do you know now that you didn't know before?
- Which idea really made you think?
- What skills have you used throughout the lesson?
- Is it important to agree on definitions together?
- What questions are you still thinking about?

## Ideas for Transfer

Students consider who has responsibility for key historical events such as the outbreak of the First World War and the Second World War. They could examine and evaluate primary and secondary resources.

Your students could produce an article for their school magazine that explores the importance of taking responsibility for your actions.

Ask your students to create a podcast that challenges different individuals and authorities on their responsibility for climate change, poverty or knife crime.

# WWW•EBI

EBI – Even Better If . . .

# Do We Feel Sympathy for Scrooge in Stave 1 of *A Christmas Carol?*

**KEY CONCEPT:** Sympathy

**KEY SKILLS:** Drawing inferences
Citing textual evidence
Analysing character development
Analysing author's word choice

# Do We Feel Sympathy for Scrooge in Stave 1 of *A Christmas Carol?*

## OVERVIEW:

This lesson will enhance students' knowledge and understanding of the character Scrooge and how he is presented to the reader. It is important for students to have read and understood the events of Stave 1 in *A Christmas Carol* so they can access this lesson.

## KEY CONCEPT:

Sympathy

## KEY WORDS:

Sorrow, pity, comfort, solace, understanding, empathy, consideration, kindness, kind-heartedness, tenderness, warmth, distress, caring, sensitivity and agreement.

## LEARNING INTENTION:

To understand how the reader reacts to the presentation of Scrooge.

## SUCCESS CRITERIA:

We can do the following:

- Discuss and explore our understanding of the word 'sympathy'.

- Examine the reasons why we may/may not feel sympathy for someone.

- Explore and discuss the ways in which a reader might react to the presentation of a character.

- Evaluate evidence from the text.

- Track the changes in a character from the start of a chapter to the end of a chapter.

- Decide if the reader feels sympathy for a main character, using evidence from the text to justify our ideas.

## STRATEGIES USED:

Concept Target

Fortune Line

# 1. IDENTIFY IMPORTANT CONCEPTS

Some of the key areas to investigate within and around the concept of 'sympathy' are the following:

- Rich and poor
- Inequality
- Life in the Victorian era
- Suffering
- Responsibility
- Philanthropy
- Greed
- Regret

# 2. CHALLENGE STUDENTS' UNDERSTANDING OF THE CONCEPT

Here are some examples of cognitive conflict we expect your students to experience:

| Opinion | Conflicting Opinion |
|---|---|
| We should feel sympathy for people who are suffering. | I can't feel sympathy for a murderer who is being punished for their crime. |
| Everyone should receive sympathy when they are going through a difficult time. | Not everyone desires sympathy; some people just want privacy. |
| The capacity to feel sympathy is a human behaviour. | If I am upset or unwell my dog shows sympathy towards me by laying its head in my lap. |
| You need to know and like someone in order to feel sympathy towards them. | I feel sympathy for the homeless people on the streets whom I neither like nor dislike as I do not know them. |
| The ability to sympathise is a learned behaviour that you develop only with age and guidance. | Babies as young as 18 months demonstrate sympathy by crying when they hear another baby crying. |

## Questions for Challenge

- What is sympathy?
- Is sympathy important?
- What makes us feel sympathy for someone?
- When should we be sympathetic?
- How should we show our sympathy?

- How should we feel when we are sympathetic?
- How do we know if someone needs/deserves our sympathy?
- Do some people deserve more sympathy than others?
- Does everyone deserve our sympathy?
- What would happen if we weren't sympathetic to others?
- How do we treat someone sympathetically?
- Do we need to like someone to show sympathy?
- Can we show sympathy for someone who refuses support and friendship?
- What is the limit of the amount of sympathy we are capable of giving?
- What makes someone deserving of sympathy?
- Does it always make you a bad person if you don't offer sympathy?
- To what extent do you need to be able to understand somebody to be able to sympathise with them?
- To what extent are sympathy and compassion the same thing?
- What if there was no such thing as sympathy?
- What's the difference between sympathy and pity?
- What's the difference between sympathy and empathy?
- How is feeling sadness towards someone's situation the same as or different from feeling sympathy?
- Should we/can we feel sympathy for those who treat others badly?
- Should we feel sympathy for criminals?
- Do strong people need sympathy?
- Should we always feel sympathy for those in need?
- Should we ever feel sympathy for someone who has enough money?
- What if we felt sympathy for everyone?
- What if we never felt sympathy towards anyone?
- Should we always feel sympathy for someone who doesn't have enough money?
- Do we need to understand a person's actions and feelings to be able to feel sympathy for them?
- Should we always feel sympathy for someone who is upset?
- Should we never feel sympathy for happy people?
- Should we always feel sympathy for those who are lonely?
- Is sympathy always an act of kindness?
- Do we show sympathy to support others or to show we are a good person?
- Can showing sympathy ever be a bad thing?
- When shouldn't we feel sympathy for people?
- Can we pretend to be sympathetic?
- Should we pretend to be sympathetic?
- Should we give sympathy even if somebody doesn't want it?

# 3. CONSTRUCT UNDERSTANDING

## Activity 1: Concept Target

Distribute **Activity 1 resource cards** to pairs/small groups.

In pairs/groups, distribute a Concept Target template or ask your students to create their own. In their pairs/groups, your students should work through each card/image to decide how close it is to the concept of 'sympathy' at the centre of the target.

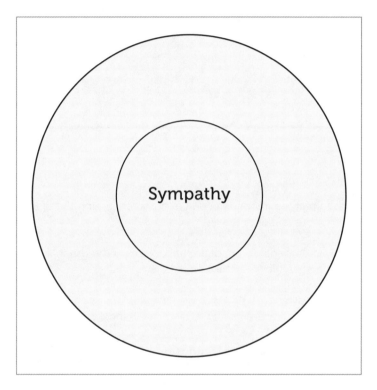

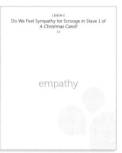

Some of the key thinking you may wish to explore with your students are as follows:

- Does sympathy need to be expressed verbally?
- Are small children equally capable of showing sympathy?
- Are animals capable of expressing sympathy?
- Can you only have sympathy for real people and real events?
- Can gestures be expressions of sympathy in themselves or does the sympathy lie in the thought behind this gesture?
- What role does body language and/or tone of voice have in the expression of sympathy?

It is also useful to return to some of the questions used in Stage 2 to help your students to secure their understanding of the concept.

## Activity 2: Fortune Line

Divide your students into small groups. Give them the Fortune Line first, then give them the associated set of statements from the **Activity 2 resources**. The Fortune Line provided is blank for your students to plot the events themselves. The x-axis refers to time and the y-axis is apathy to sympathy.

Do We Feel Sympathy for Scrooge in Stave 1 of *A Christmas Carol*?

Challenging LEARNING     47

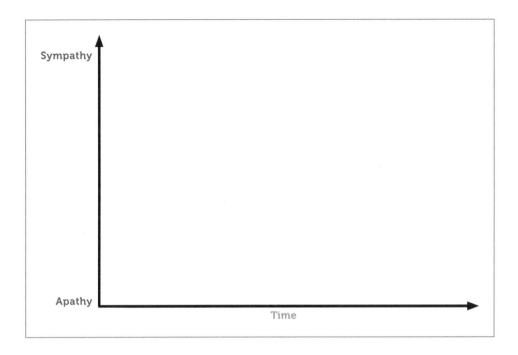

Ask each group to plot the information on the graph according to the time and the level of sympathy felt by the reader in Stave 1.

It is helpful for your students to annotate their ideas on the graph as they position the statements in the places they feel they should be.

Once your students have completed their Fortune Line, they can share their findings with other groups to identify similarities and differences in the positioning of each quotation.

### Questions to Promote Further Dialogue

- What do we learn about Scrooge's personal circumstances in the text?
- Does the death of Jacob Marley affect our sympathies for Scrooge?
- Do we feel sympathy for Scrooge because he spends time alone?
- Should Scrooge's treatment of others affect our view of him?
- If we feel sympathy for Scrooge, what do we feel for the clerk, Bob Cratchit?
- Why doesn't Scrooge want to visit his nephew during Christmas?
- If Scrooge had given money to the men who called, would we have more sympathy for him?
- Is Scrooge a likeable character? Do we need to like Scrooge to feel sympathy for him?
- Is Scrooge happy? Should this alter our sympathy for him?
- Does Dickens want the reader to sympathise with Scrooge? How do you know this? Look at the use of language and the sentence structures.

- What do we know about Dickens' political/social views? Does this help us understand Scrooge better?

- Does our sympathy with Scrooge change when he sees Marley's ghost?

- Has Scrooge changed by the end of Stave 1?

## Adaptation

Reduce the number of cards or resources the students are categorising at any one time.

## Extension

Ask your students to create a Fortune Line on sympathy for the whole book or for another specified chapter. It may be worthwhile to allocate the remaining staves to specified groups who can then share their findings with the rest of the class (Jigsaw Grouping).

Having explored this concept, you could ask your students to plan and write an essay in response to the key question.

# 4. CONSIDER THE LEARNING JOURNEY

At the end of the activity it is usual to encourage your students to review their learning journey and the thinking process they have engaged in throughout the session.

This can include reflection on the thinking that has taken place to this point and a summary and conclusion of the new understanding reached.

Explicit reference to Learning Intentions and Success Criteria is a good starting point for this reflection, but it is also helpful to return to and re-examine some key questions:

- Do you have a deeper or better understanding of the concept of 'sympathy'?

- Which parts of the lesson helped you to decide and/or change your knowledge and understanding of sympathy?

- What questions do you still have?

- What would you like to investigate further?

- Should we feel sympathy for Scrooge in Stave 1?

## Ideas for Transfer

Ask your students to investigate if we feel sympathy for other characters in books by Charles Dickens, such as Miss Havisham from *Great Expectations* or Fagin from *Oliver Twist.* Students could record their ideas using a Venn Diagram or a Fortune Line.

Your students could create their own character who provokes sympathy in the reader.

Ask your students to create their own online advertisement/short film clip that uses sympathy bias to persuade the audience.

# WWW•EBI

## WWW – What Worked Well . . .

## EBI – Even Better If . . .

LESSON

# 3

# How Are Dreams Presented in *Jane Eyre*?

**KEY CONCEPT:** Dreams

**KEY SKILLS:** Analysing author's word choice
Analysing point of view
Analysing the development of theme
Citing textual evidence
Comparing and contrasting

# How Are Dreams Presented in *Jane Eyre*?

**OVERVIEW:**

This lesson will enhance students' knowledge and understanding on the presentation and role of dreams in the novel *Jane Eyre*. It is important for students to have a secure understanding of the novel so they can access this lesson.

**KEY CONCEPT:**

Dreams

**KEY WORDS:**

Dreams, wishes, fantasies, goal setting, aspirations, happiness, supernatural, fairy tales, love and romance, imaginative, reality, wonderful, perfect, daydream, successful, optimism, memory, nightmares, flashback, hopes, visions, hallucination, superstition, prophecy, memory and apparitions.

**LEARNING INTENTION:**

To understand how dreams are presented in *Jane Eyre*.

**SUCCESS CRITERIA:**

We can do the following:

- Discuss and explore what we understand by dreams.

- Apply our understanding of dreams to identify examples in *Jane Eyre*.

- Consider and explore Charlotte Brontë's representation of dreams in the novel.

- Evaluate the evidence of dreams in *Jane Eyre* to explore how they are presented.

**STRATEGIES USED:**

Concept Target

Sorting and Classifying

# 1. IDENTIFY IMPORTANT CONCEPTS

Some of the key areas to investigate within and around the concept of 'dreams' are the following:

- The definition of dreams
- Happiness
- Fear
- Fairy tales
- Romanticism
- The supernatural
- Aspirations
- Love and romance
- Consciousness
- Gothic tales

# 2. CHALLENGE STUDENTS' UNDERSTANDING OF THE CONCEPT

Here are some examples of cognitive conflict we expect your students to experience:

| Opinion | Conflicting Opinion |
| --- | --- |
| Dreaming is something I do when I'm asleep. | I often dream when I'm awake about things I'd like to do. |
| Dreams are just fantasy. | Dreams are often rooted in reality. |
| Dreams never come true. | Dreams can become a reality if you make a plan to fulfil them. |
| He'll never go anywhere in life, he's just a dreamer. | He dreamt about it, he made it happen and now he's living the dream. |
| Dreams are a wonderful part of sleeping. | Bad dreams ruin sleep. |

## Questions for Challenge

- What is a dream?
- How do we know what a dream is?
- What makes something a dream?
- Who decides if something is a dream or real?
- How do we know when we are dreaming?

- Why do we dream?

- What do we know about the different types of dreams?

- Is it possible to dream and be awake at the same time?

- Socrates asks, 'How can you determine whether at this moment we are sleeping, and all our thoughts are a dream; or whether we are awake, and talking to one another in the waking state?'

- What are our dreams based on?

- What is a daydream?

- Why do we daydream?

- How do we know if we are daydreaming?

- Do we choose to daydream?

- Can we choose our daydream?

- Can we daydream at night?

- What's the difference between a daydream and a sleeping dream?

- Is daydreaming the same as thinking?

- Is dreaming the same as thinking?

- What do dreams tell us?

- What do we learn from our dreams?

- What if we didn't dream?

- How do we see dreams?

- Are any dreams achievable?

- What would make a dream perfect?

- When are our dreams more important than real events?

- What can we do in our dreams that we can't do anywhere else?

- Are you ever the same person in your dreams as you are in reality?

- Can we control our dreams?

- What is the difference between a dream and a vision?

- What is the difference between a dream and a flashback?

- What is a fantasy?

- What is the difference between a fantasy and a dream?

- What is the difference between a dream and a nightmare?

- Are daydreams aspirational visions of who we are?

- If we imagine our lives in the future, are we dreaming?

- Do you only daydream when you are unhappy?

- How do our dreams change us?

- Is it only people with an active imagination who daydream?

- What is the difference between dreams and aspirations?

- Sigmund Freud believed that the content of our dreams reveals our unconscious desires. How much do you agree with this idea?

# 3. CONSTRUCT UNDERSTANDING

## Activity 1: Concept Target

Distribute the **Activity 1 resource cards** to pairs or small groups.

Distribute Concept Target templates or ask your students to create their own. Your students should consider each card and decide how close it is to the concept of 'dreams' at the centre of the target.

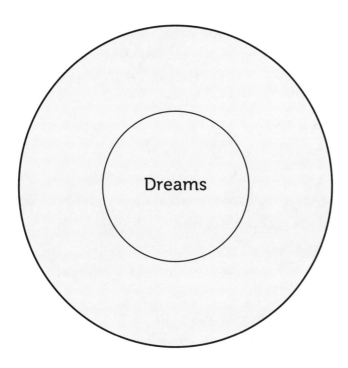

**Download the activity cards at http://resources.corwin.com/learningchallengelessons**

Ask your students to justify the position of the cards and to explore each other's reasoning. It is also important to encourage your students to move the cards at any point if they change their minds.

Some of the key thinking you may wish to explore with your students are as follows:

- How would you define a dream?
- Are there any words that aren't included that you think would help our understanding of dreams?
- How has your understanding of dreams changed?

## Activity 2: Sorting and Classifying

Introduce the following key question:

**How are dreams presented in *Jane Eyre*?**

Distribute the **Activity 2 resource cards**. Give your students time to read them and identify the type of dream each one depicts.

They can use the categories from the **Activity 1 resource cards** as the headings for this.

It will be useful for your students to revisit the novel and explore the events surrounding the quotations and find other examples of dreams or quotations in the text.

Encourage your students to visit other groups to see how the cards have been sorted and classified.

## Questions for Further Dialogue

- What does this Sorting and Classifying activity reveal about the presentation of dreams?
- Which cards were difficult to place? Why was this?
- Which cards belonged to more than one category? Why was this?
- Are some dreams more prevalent than others? What could be the reasons for this?
- Do you agree or disagree with how other groups have sorted and classified the resource cards? Explain your reasons for this.

## Questions on *Jane Eyre*

- How do we identify dreams in the novel?
- What do we learn about the different types of dreams in *Jane Eyre*?
- What are the similarities and differences in these types of dreams?
- How does Charlotte Brontë use dreams in her novel?
- What does Jane Eyre daydream about?
- How do we learn about Jane Eyre's thoughts and feelings?
- What are Jane Eyre's dreams for the future?
- What do dreams tell us about Jane Eyre?
- Which of Jane Eyre's dreams are based on real events?
- When Jane Eyre's dreams come true, should they have been labelled as something other than a dream?
- How important are dreams to Jane's future?
- How important are dreams to Mr Rochester?
- How are Jane Eyre and Mr Rochester controlled by their dreams?
- What are the similarities and differences in the ways that Jane Eyre and Mr Rochester respond to dreams?
- In what ways do dreams change Jane Eyre?
- What if we didn't learn about Jane's dreams? How would this affect our understanding of the novel?
- What are the similarities and differences between Jane's daydreams and night dreams?
- Should we view Jane Eyre's life as a fairytale in the same way as we would see Cinderella? Does this affect our answer to the question?
- How does Jane Eyre view Mr Rochester?

- Does the love and romance between Jane and Mr Rochester mean that the novel should be regarded as a story of dreams?

- Why was Jane Eyre unsettled by her dreams before she was due to marry Mr Rochester?

- Jane Eyre's suffering and struggles are rooted in reality. Does this mean that the dreams are just a form of escapism?

## Adaptation

Reduce the number of cards or resources they are categorising at any one time.

Provide a summary of each chapter in the novel.

Provide a timeline of the key events in the novel.

## Extension

Provide your students with fewer quotations in **Activity 2** so they must find their own examples in the text.

Ask your students to create a Living Graph to explore the importance of dreams across time.

Ask your students to identify nine key dreams from the novel and then rank their importance using a Diamond Ranking format.

Having explored this concept, you could ask your students to plan and write an essay in response to the key question.

# 4. CONSIDER THE LEARNING JOURNEY

At the end of the activity it is usual to encourage the students to review their learning journey and the thinking progress they have engaged in throughout the session.

This can include reflection on the thinking that has taken place up to this point and a summary and conclusion of the new understanding reached.

Explicit reference to Learning Intentions and Success Criteria is a good starting point for this reflection, but it is also helpful to return to and re-examine some key questions:

- How are dreams presented in *Jane Eyre*?

- Do you have a deeper understanding of the concept of 'dreams'?

- Has anyone changed their mind about what dreams are?

- What have you learned about the presentation of dreams in *Jane Eyre*?

- Which idea really made you think?

- What questions do you still have?

## Ideas for Transfer

Ask your students to explore the presentation of dreams in the text *Wide Sargasso Sea*, which was written by Jean Rhys who was inspired by *Jane Eyre*.

Compare the presentation of dreams in the Brontë novels with other works such as *Oliver Twist* and *Great Expectations* by Charles Dickens.

Students could be encouraged to consider what their dreams and aspirations for the future are. Goal-setting activities could be used to enable students to make these dreams a reality. Students who prefer a visual representation of their dreams and aspirations could create a dream chart and find images or quotes from magazines or the internet to create a collage to represent their dreams.

Challenge your students to create a short story that uses dreams as a literary device.

To explore the concept of 'dreams' in different mediums, ask your students to pick a dream from the resource cards and discuss how they would portray this on stage or on film.

# WWW•EBI

## WWW – What Worked Well . . .

## EBI – Even Better If . . .

# Does Heathcliff Become More or Less Monstrous Over the Course of the Novel *Wuthering Heights*?

**KEY CONCEPT:** Monster

**KEY SKILLS:** Analysing character development
Citing textual evidence
Crafting an argument
Demonstrating understanding of figurative language and nuance
Determining figurative and connotative meanings of words
Evaluating evidence

# Does Heathcliff Become More or Less Monstrous Over the Course of the Novel *Wuthering Heights*?

## OVERVIEW:

This lesson on *Wuthering Heights* by Emily Brontë will enhance students' knowledge and understanding of the character development of Heathcliff throughout the novel.

## KEY CONCEPT:

Monster

## KEY WORDS:

Monster, beast, villain, supernatural, evil, mythical, treacherous, brute, fiend, ogre, devil, demon, barbarian, savage, rascal, imp, wretch, mischief-maker, rogue, horror, scallywag, monstrosity, freak, goliath, gigantic, unnatural, revenge and wildness.

## LEARNING INTENTION:

To be able to recognise whether Heathcliff becomes more or less monstrous throughout the novel *Wuthering Heights*.

## SUCCESS CRITERIA:

We can do the following:

- Explore and discuss our understanding of the term 'monster'.

- Identify the key characteristics of 'monstrous' behaviour.

- Interpret extracts and evaluate the author's use of language to judge how monstrous Heathcliff's appearance, behaviour and actions are.

- Track the development of a character from the start of a novel to the end of a novel using a Living Graph.

- Construct a concluding argument explaining the relationship between the novel's development and the monstrous behaviour of Heathcliff.

## STRATEGIES USED:

Sorting and Classifying

Living Graph

# 1. IDENTIFY IMPORTANT CONCEPTS

Some of the key areas to investigate within and around the concept of 'monster' in *Wuthering Heights* are the following:

- Attitudes towards the supernatural in the 19th century vs. attitudes to the supernatural in society today
- Supernatural genre
- The Gothic Tradition
- Symbolism
- Animal imagery
- Weather
- Romanticism
- Horror genre
- Religion
- Revenge
- Love
- Nature vs. culture

## Activity 1: Provoke the Discussion Through Sorting and Classifying

Distribute the **Activity 1 resource cards** to small groups or pairs and ask your students to sort and classify the cards into two sets as follows:

'Monster' and 'Not a monster'.

They should share the criteria they are using to sort and classify.

Ask your students to decide on a list of five criteria that would help them decide whether a character is a monster. They should share their criteria with the rest of the class.

It is likely that your students will not recognise all the figures in the resources, which could allow them to research the concept further and feed their results back to the class.

**Download the activity cards at http://resources.corwin.com/ learningchallengelessons**

# 2. CHALLENGE STUDENTS' UNDERSTANDING OF THE CONCEPT

Here are some examples of cognitive conflict we expect your students to experience:

| Opinion | Conflicting Opinion |
|---|---|
| Monstrous people are born that way. | Monstrous people develop in response to the conditions around them. |
| Human behaviour can be interpreted and understood. | Monstrous human behaviour exceeds our understanding. |
| Monsters are without morals. | Monsters can exhibit moral behaviour. For example, Adolf Hitler was a strong defender of the institution of marriage. |

*(Continued)*

(Continued)

| Opinion | Conflicting Opinion |
|---|---|
| You can tell that someone is a monster by their appearance. | Monsters look the same as any other person. |
| A monster is defined by their actions alone. | Someone is only a monster if others judge them to be so. |
| It's obvious to tell if someone is a monster. | Monsters can exist anonymously within our communities. |

### Questions for Challenge

- What do we understand by the term 'monster' when applied to a person?
- Who decides if someone is a monster?
- How are monsters created?
- What forms do monsters take in real life?
- Are monsters always evil?
- Is someone born a monster?
- What would cause a human to be called a monster?
- What is the difference between a monster and a villain?
- What behaviour defines a monster?
- Does a monster always behave badly?
- Does a monster always exhibit monstrous behaviour?
- When do monsters have morals?
- When might monsters have a purpose?
- When could monsters ever be capable of love?
- To what degree are monsters something to be afraid of?
- How important is appearance in defining a monster?
- Do we always know if someone is a monster?
- To what extent are monsters defined by the power they yield?
- How is it possible for a monster to also be a hero?
- What is the difference between being a monster and behaving monstrously?
- Where do monsters exist in our society?
- Can monsters change or does our perception of them change?
- Do we ever feel sympathy for monsters? Why?

# 3. CONSTRUCT UNDERSTANDING

## Activity 2: Living Graph

Divide your students into pairs or small groups and ask them to create a Living Graph as the example below.

online resources

Download the activity cards at http://resources.corwin.com/learningchallengelessons

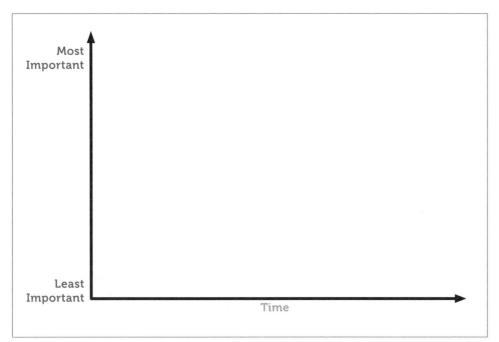

LESSON 4
Does Heathcliff Become More or Less Monstrous Over the Course of the Novel *Wuthering Heights*?
2.1

'He got on to the bed, and wrenched open the lattice, bursting, as he pulled at it, into an uncontrollable passion of tears. "Come in! come in!" he sobbed. "Cathy, do come. Oh, do – ONCE more!"'

Heathcliff
Chapter 3

LESSON 4
Does Heathcliff Become More or Less Monstrous Over the Course of the Novel *Wuthering Heights*?
2.3

'I tried to close his eyes: to extinguish, if possible, that frightful, life-like gaze of exultation before any one else beheld it. They would not shut: they seemed to sneer at my attempts.'

Nelly Dean explaining what happened when she found Heathcliff dead.
Chapter 34

Your students should analyse and interpret the extracts on the **Activity 2 resource cards** and decide where that piece of evidence would be placed on the graph. They must take into account the chronology of the evidence as well as how monstrous they judge Heathcliff to be at this stage.

## Questions to Promote Further Dialogue

- What makes one act more monstrous than another?

- How does the character's age affect our interpretation of what qualifies as 'monstrous' behaviour?

- How important is Heathcliff's appearance in depicting him as a monster?

- What is the impact of the author's use of language on whether we perceive Heathcliff to be a monster or not?

- How does the development of key events in the novel make Heathcliff more or less monstrous?

- Does love make Heathcliff more or less monstrous?

- At which point in the novel is Heathcliff at his most monstrous?

- At which point in the novel is Heathcliff at his least monstrous?

- What does this tell us about the character development of Heathcliff throughout the course of the novel?

- To what extent can we trust the evidence in the extracts?

- To what extent is the development of Heathcliff's monstrous behaviour fundamental to the success of the novel?

### Adaptation

Use a smaller number of cards for each activity.

To provide more guidance on the time frame of the novel and phases of Heathcliff's life, you could provide the following stages to be used on the x-axis:

- Prologue
- Childhood of Heathcliff
- Maturity of Heathcliff
- Epilogue

### Extension

For **Activity 1**, ask your students to create their own list of monsters that can be found in books and films.

Use the **Activity 2 resource cards** as a Sorting and Classifying activity. Ask your students to sort through the cards looking for different features of language and devices to explore Heathcliff's characteristics. For example, your students could be asked to find the metaphors, symbols, adjectives and animals used to describe him.

Allocate a resource card from **Activity 2** to each student or pair. Each student or pair must create a paragraph that analyses and explores how the use of language, literary devices and sentence structure from their resource card reflects Heathcliff's monstrous qualities. Before they begin their analysis, it would be beneficial for your students to have seen an example of what a good one looks like (WAGOLL). This could be followed by peer assessment and feedback.

Your students could construct an essay answer to the key activity question.

## 4. CONSIDER THE LEARNING JOURNEY

At the end of the activity it is usual to encourage your students to review their learning journey and the thinking process they have engaged in throughout the session.

This can include reflection on the thinking that has taken place to this point and a summary and conclusion of the new understanding reached.

Explicit reference to Learning Intentions and Success Criteria is a good starting point for this reflection.

To encourage the students to review their learning journey and their thinking progress, students could be asked to consider where they would place themselves on an Opinion Line according to the following statements:

**Heathcliff becomes more monstrous over the course of the novel.**

**Heathcliff becomes less monstrous over the course of the novel.**

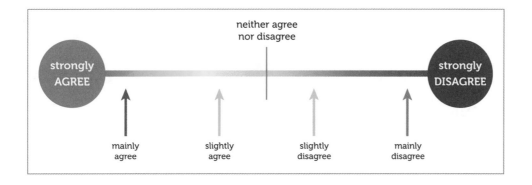

Each student should construct a short argument for each statement, outlining their key reasons for their judgement. Their arguments should be supported and justified by references to some of the key evidence from the novel. Your students can place a name card for themselves on the line in a position representative of their argument. You can select names, depending on where they are positioned on the line, to share their arguments with the whole group. The reasons and justifications should be questioned and their position challenged by comparison with other arguments and alternative viewpoints.

## Possible Questions to Review the Learning Journey

- Has anyone changed their mind about what defines someone as a monster?
- What do you now understand about people labelled as monsters?
- Which ideas really made you think?
- What skills have you used throughout the lesson?
- Is it important to agree on definitions together?
- What questions are you still thinking about?
- How has your opinion of Heathcliff changed over the course of this lesson?
- Does Heathcliff become more or less monstrous over the course of *Wuthering Heights*?

## Ideas for Transfer

Using the criteria for a monster decided in **Activity 1**, ask your students to investigate if their five criteria apply to other monster characters in literature or films.

Students could compare the presentation of Heathcliff and Frankenstein's monster using a Venn Diagram.

To develop a more historical view of the concept, ask your students to explore the presentation of monsters in literature from different eras. A useful starting point could be the presentation of monsters in Old English literature such as Grendel in *Beowulf*.

Ask your students to explore the role of monsters in Shakespeare's plays. A useful starting point could be Caliban in *The Tempest*.

Your students could compare the portrayal of Heathcliff by different actors in the various film versions of *Wuthering Heights* to determine how each one presented his monstrous nature.

# WWW•EBI

**WWW – What Worked Well . . .**

**EBI – Even Better If . . .**

# Does Louisa May Alcott's Novel *Little Women* Accept or Challenge Gender Stereotypes?

**KEY CONCEPT:** Gender Stereotypes

**KEY SKILLS:** Crafting an argument
Citing textual evidence
Analysing how individuals and ideas are portrayed in a text
Evaluating arguments
Determining an author's point of view

# Does Louisa May Alcott's Novel *Little Women* Accept or Challenge Gender Stereotypes?

## OVERVIEW:

This lesson will enhance students' knowledge and understanding of how the female characters are represented in the novel *Little Women* and to what extent they are stereotypical of that time. Students need to have read and studied the novel before taking part in these lesson activities.

## KEY CONCEPT:

Gender stereotypes

## KEY WORDS:

Gender, stereotypes, feminism, women's rights, masculinity, patriarchal, human rights, suffrage, Victorian values, independence, family, portrayal, representation, personal growth and labels.

## LEARNING INTENTION:

To understand the portrayal of gender stereotypes in Louisa May Alcott's novel *Little Women*.

## SUCCESS CRITERIA:

We can do the following:

- Identify and explore how gender is represented in a range of media texts and literature.

- Define what we understand by a gender stereotype.

- Create a list of the typical characteristics we would expect to find in a female stereotype.

- Compare the characteristics of female stereotypes in the Victorian period with the modern day.

- Explore and examine the presentation of the key female characters in *Little Women*.

- Assess how the presentation of the key characters challenges and/or accepts gender stereotypes.

## STRATEGIES USED:

Diamond Ranking

Jigsaw Groups

Concept Target

Mystery

# 1. IDENTIFY IMPORTANT CONCEPTS

Some of the key areas to investigate within and around the concept of 'gender stereotypes' are the following:

- A definition of stereotype
- Examples of gender stereotypes over time
- Gender stereotypes across cultures
- Feminist movement
- Equal rights
- Gender stereotypes in the media
- Masculinity
- Femininity
- Patriarchy

## Activity 1: Provoke the Discussion

Provide your students with a range of media and commercial resources, for example, catalogues, magazines, newspapers, media clips, film posters, advertisements, etc.

In pairs/groups, ask your students to investigate the representation of females and males in these sources. This investigation can result in a collage or an artistic depiction of their findings. You could provide categories for the students to focus on, such as appearance, clothing, colours, actions and attitudes.

To develop the investigation further, you could ask your students to consider the representation of men and women in the literature texts they may have studied, for example, Romeo and Juliet or Curley and Curley's wife from *Of Mice and Men*.

- How are males and females represented in these sources?
- Are there any similarities or differences in the way the sources represent males and females?
- Can you spot any patterns in the language used to represent men and women in these sources?
- To what extent does the media influence our understanding of male and female roles?
- What has been the most interesting find from your investigations?
- What have you learnt about the stereotyping of males and females in this exercise?
- Do you have any stories or experiences of stereotyping?

Ask your students to complete the following sentences to help define and clarify their understanding of stereotypes.

**A stereotype is . . .**

**A female stereotype is . . .**

**A male stereotype is . . .**

# 2. CHALLENGE STUDENTS' UNDERSTANDING OF THE CONCEPT

Here are some examples of cognitive conflict we expect your students to experience:

| Opinion | Conflicting Opinion |
|---|---|
| Your gender is determined by your sex. | You may physically resemble one sex but feel and relate to the opposite sex much more. |
| Gender differences are determined by biology. | Gender differences are a social construct. |
| There are obvious differences between girls and boys. | Many women seem quite masculine and many men seem quite feminine. |
| There is no advantage in having boys' toys and girls' toys. | Toy manufacturers boost their sales by deliberately producing gender-specific toys. |
| There should not be discrimination according to gender. | In many sports it is thought to be unfair for men to compete against women. |
| Gender discrimination is illegal in many countries. | Many of these same countries use positive discrimination to counter inequality. |

## Questions for Challenge

- What is gender?
- What is a stereotype?
- What is a gender stereotype?
- What and who do we stereotype?
- What makes something or someone a stereotype?
- How do we know what a gender stereotype is?
- Who decides what a gender stereotype is?
- Can we always know if something or someone is a gender stereotype?
- Who is more likely to understand gender stereotyping, the person being stereotyped or the person doing the stereotyping?
- Would a stereotype be a real person?
- Where do gender stereotypes come from?
- Why are gender stereotypes used?
- How and why do stereotypes change?
- What makes a stereotype an 'over-simplified image'?
- How are stereotypes important?
- How are gender stereotypes important or valuable?
- How are gender stereotypes truthful?
- Should we never believe stereotypes?
- When are gender stereotypes fair?
- When are gender stereotypes true?
- What if stereotypes didn't exist?
- How does a stereotype make you similar to or different from others?

- Is it possible to be stereotypical and different at the same time?

- What is the difference between a character being typical and stereotypical?

- What is the difference between being a stereotype and being stereotypical?

- To what extent are gender stereotypes representative of modern-day attitudes and views of women?

- How important is appearance when exploring gender stereotypes?

- What other stereotypes can you think of?

- What are the differences between gender stereotypes and gender discrimination?

- What is sexism?

- How does gender differ from sex?

- What is the relationship between sex and gender?

- How is gender stereotyping dangerous?

- What is gender mainstreaming?

- Do the books a child reads or the films a child watches influence their gender identity?

- Is gender socially constructed and culturally variable?

- What is the point of challenging gender stereotypes?

- How could the language we use reinforce or challenge gender stereotypes?

- 'The gender stereotypes introduced in childhood are reinforced throughout our lives and become self-fulfilling prophecies. Most leadership positions are held by men, so women don't expect to achieve them, and that becomes one of the reasons they don't.' Sheryl Sandberg. To what extent do you agree?

- 'I am neither a man nor a woman but an author.' Charlotte Brontë. What is our most important defining characteristic? Gender? Occupation? Age? Sexuality?

# 3. CONSTRUCT UNDERSTANDING

**Activity 2: Diamond Ranking x2**

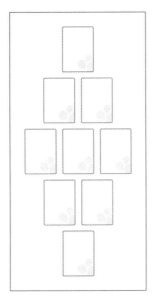

Based on their discussions from the previous activity, ask your students to create a list of the characteristics of the following:

(1) A female stereotype in society today.

Your students must now write each of these characteristics on separate pieces of paper or card. They should then rank these according to their importance. Encourage them to discuss and explore the positioning of each characteristic, justifying the placement of each with key reasons.

To appreciate the historical and social context surrounding the novel, your students should now re-rank the characteristics according to the following:

(2) Female stereotypes in the 1800s.

This activity will encourage your students to consider and research the representation of women during this period, exploring newspapers/magazines/films, etc.

### Questions to Promote Further Dialogue

- How did you decide on the most important characteristic?
- Why are some characteristics more important than others?
- Which characteristics have changed position for the 1800s and why?
- Which cards have stayed in the same position and why?
- How does this activity help us understand the female stereotypes in *Little Women*?

### Activity 3: Jigsaw Grouping

Divide your students into five groups. These are the home groups. Adjust the group size if the class size is smaller/larger than 25.

Each group will be allocated a female character from the novel. The female characters to be explored are:

- Josephine March
- Meg March
- Beth March
- Amy March
- Marmee

Give each home group the **Activity 3 character worksheet**, which contains labelled spaces for the students to complete. Alternatively, you could ask your students to present this information in a manner of their choosing.

Your students must use the completion of this sheet to help them to answer the question:

**Is (*name of character*) a gender stereotype?**

Your students must find evidence from the novel and contribute their own ideas on the following areas:

- Appearance
- Thoughts

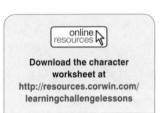

online
resources
**Download the character worksheet at**
http://resources.corwin.com/
learningchallengelessons

- Actions

- Attitudes and behaviour

- How others view them

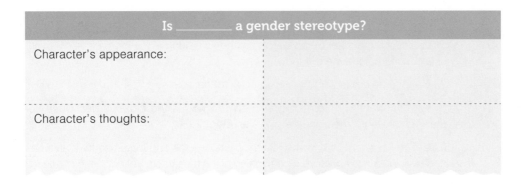

| Is _____ a gender stereotype? | |
|---|---|
| Character's appearance: | |
| Character's thoughts: | |

In their home groups, they must investigate if their character is a stereotype by looking at the areas above and using their ideas from **Activities 1** and **2**.

Once each home group feels they have a good understanding of how their character is presented, they must share their understanding with the rest of the groups in the class.

Ask each student in the group to number themselves one to five. Now ask Person 1 from each group to sit together, and Person 2, etc. These new groups are the away groups. Each member of the away group takes it in turns to present their ideas about how their character is presented. By sharing the information they have studied, the whole group gets a broader picture of stereotyping with the five main female characters.

Once all the information has been shared in the away group, the students can return to their home group and share what they have learned about the other characters.

### Activity 4: Concept Target

Distribute a Concept Target template or ask each group to create their own. In their pairs/ groups, your students should now use the information from **Activity 3** to decide how close each character is to the central concept of a female stereotype.

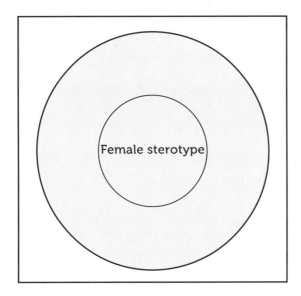

Encourage your students to share their thinking and justify the position of each character using evidence from **Activity 3**.

Some of the key thinking you may wish to explore with your students are as follows:

- Which character was difficult to place? Why was this?

- Which character was easier to place? Why was this?

- Should every character be a stereotype and so belong in the inner circle? Is every fictional character a stereotype?

- Why are some characters nearer the target than others?

- Is age important in determining stereotype? Meg is the oldest sister. Does her maturity make her more or less of a stereotype?

- *Little Women* shows us how the March sisters change and mature in their attitudes and behaviour. How does your positioning of each character reflect these changes?

## Activity 5: Mystery

Divide the class into groups of 3 or 4 and distribute the **Activity 5 resource cards** (which can be found online). Your students must now bring all their ideas together to answer the following key question:

**Does Louisa May Alcott's novel *Little Women* accept or challenge gender stereotypes?**

It is useful to support your students when they are sorting through the information in front of them. This can help them to interpret and handle the information more easily, and reconstruct their thinking in order to reach an understanding.

This Consider Chart can help them assimilate their thinking.

| Evidence that shows *Little Women* accepts female stereotypes. | Evidence that shows *Little Women* challenges female stereotypes. | Evidence that is not relevant. |
|---|---|---|
| | | |

Our conclusion is . . .

The key reasons for this are . . .

### Questions to Promote Further Dialogue

- How do we know if Alcott is challenging female stereotypes?

- How do we know if Alcott is accepting female stereotypes?

- What might the title of the book reveal about the stereotypes in the novel? Why does Alcott use the adjective 'little'?

- It is reported that Alcott based her novel on her own childhood experiences. How does this affect our views of stereotypes in the novel?

- Would Alcott have had a choice in her portrayal of female characters?

- Who was Alcott writing her book for?

- Why is the sequel to *Little Women* called *Good Wives*? How does this affect our view of female stereotypes in *Little Women*?

- Why might Alcott use female stereotypes in the novel?

- Why is *Little Women* dominated by female characters?

- How do we know if Alcott is challenging stereotypes?

- If stereotypes are based on truth, should they be challenged?

- Does Alcott challenge female stereotypes through both public and private spheres?

- Why does the writer refer to Jo's behaviour as 'boyish' or 'gentlemanly'? Does this reinforce or challenge female stereotypes?

- How does Jo's rebellion suggest that Alcott was challenging stereotypes?

- Should we view Jo's refusal to conform as childish and petulant or as an attempt to challenge stereotypes?

- Does the fact that most of the sisters are married by the end of the book reinforce or challenge female stereotypes? If Jo had refused to marry, would this have been clear evidence that Alcott was challenging stereotypes?

- How should we view Marmee's role and influence in the novel considering the patriarchal society at this time?

- Many critics have praised *Little Women* for its 'realism' and for breaking away from traditional didactic tales. To what extent do you agree with these critics and does this suggest that Alcott does challenge gender stereotypes?

- Does the omniscient narrator reinforce or challenge the stereotypes?

- *Little Women* remains a very popular novel. What might this popularity show us about female stereotypes in the novel?

## Adaptation

Fewer cards could be used, or support can be given when students are sorting through the cards.

For those students who respond to a visual stimulus, an adaptation of the novel could be shown to highlight key points or to replace certain cards.

## Extension

Include some blank cards for students to add their own commentary or quotes from the text or wider research.

To explore and track how the female characters change in the novel, ask your students to create a Living Graph, with the x-axis as time and the y-axis determining the extent to which they display stereotypical characteristics.

Using a Venn Diagram, ask your students to compare the representation of the sisters in the private sphere vs. the public sphere.

Students could write up their findings in essay form.

Having explored this concept, you could ask your students to plan and write an essay in response to the key question.

# 4. CONSIDER THE LEARNING JOURNEY

At the end of the activity it is usual to encourage your students to review their learning journey and the thinking process they have engaged in throughout the session.

This can include reflection on the thinking that has taken place up to this point and a summary and conclusion of the new understanding reached.

Explicit reference to Learning Intentions and Success Criteria is a good starting point for this reflection, but it is also helpful to return to and re-examine some key questions:

- What do you understand about gender stereotypes?
- What do you know now that you didn't know before?
- Which idea really made you think?
- Have your views of the novel or the author changed or developed?
- What questions do you still have?
- How important is an understanding of gender stereotypes?

### Ideas for Transfer

To build on your students' understanding of gender stereotypes, ask them to examine whether the novel accepts or challenges male stereotypes. **Activity 1** can be used to explore the portrayal of males in media texts and literature, followed by more focused analysis of the male characters in the novel for **Activities 2**, **3** and **4**. Your students can focus on Mr March, Mr Brooke, Frederick Bhaer and Mr Laurence.

Students could consider how their childhood experiences have affected their current gender-associated beliefs and behaviours. They could explore this by undertaking an online shopping experience and choosing toys they feel are most fitting to children of different ages, then discuss their findings in groups.

In groups students could brainstorm a list of phrases and statements commonly used to describe boys and girls, they could then evaluate their findings and enquire into why.

Students could re-imagine the novel *Little Women* by transposing it into a contemporary setting. They could create pen portraits of the key characters they've been examining within this lesson, revising these to reflect 21st-century attitudes and, potentially, identifying current stereotypes.

## Is _____ a gender stereotype?

Character's appearance:

Character's thoughts:

Character's actions:

Character's attitudes and behaviours:

The view of other characters towards them:

# WWW•EBI

## WWW – What Worked Well . . .

## EBI – Even Better If . . .

# Was Toto Dorothy's Only True Friend?

**KEY CONCEPT:** Friendship

**KEY SKILLS:** Citing textual evidence
Identifying theme
Crafting an argument

# Was Toto Dorothy's Only True Friend?

## OVERVIEW:

It would be beneficial for students to have read the book *The Wonderful Wizard of Oz* by L. Frank Baum and to have an emerging awareness of plot and characterisation.

## KEY CONCEPT:

Friendship

## KEY WORDS:

Friends, friendship, family, teamwork, self-sufficiency, self-awareness, loyalty, forgiveness, thoughtfulness, kindness, protective, loving, spiritual, joyful, happiness and commitment.

## LEARNING INTENTION:

To understand the significance of friendship within *The Wonderful Wizard of Oz*.

## SUCCESS CRITERIA:

We can do the following:

- Discuss, explore and define what we understand by the term 'friendship.'
- Evaluate the relative value of the key characteristics of friendship.
- Sort and classify information to make judgements about the relationships Dorothy forms in *The Wonderful Wizard of Oz*.
- Identify textual evidence to support our analysis and interpretations.

## STRATEGIES USED:

Diamond Ranking

Mystery

# 1. IDENTIFY IMPORTANT CONCEPTS

Some of the key areas to investigate within and around the concept of 'friendship' are the following:

- The nature of friendship
- The importance of friendship
- Age and maturity
- Sociological and economic aspects of friendship
- The psychological impact of friendship
- Happiness
- Loneliness

# 2. CHALLENGE STUDENTS' UNDERSTANDING OF THE CONCEPT

Here are some examples of cognitive conflict we expect your students to experience:

| Opinion | Conflicting Opinion |
| --- | --- |
| A friend should share everything with you. | I don't want my friends to share their germs and illnesses with me. |
| Friends are nice to each other. | Other people are nice to me but that doesn't mean they are my friend.<br>Sometimes my friend is mean to me. |
| Friends like the same things. | My friend likes some things that I don't (e.g., carrots). |
| You should have as many friends as you can get. | One very good friend is all you need. |
| A friend is someone you trust. | I trust my teacher and my doctor but they are not my friends. |
| Friends make you happy. | Someone with 700 'friends' on social media is no happier than someone with no friends on social media. |
| Friends spend time with each other. | Some friends haven't seen each other for years. |

## Questions for Challenge

- What is a friend?
- When is a friend not a friend?
- How do we know what a friend is?
- Who decides what a friend is?
- Can we always know who our friends are?

- What is a true friend?
- What makes a true friend?
- How do we know what a true friend is?
- Can anyone be a true friend?
- How can we measure friendship?
- What qualities does a true friend have?
- When does somebody become a friend?
- When does somebody become a true friend?
- How do you know you have friends?
- Should we only look for true friends?
- Should we always look after our friends?
- Should our friends always look after us?
- Should true friends always put you first?
- Should true friends always make us happy?
- Should we always miss true friends?
- Do true friends never let us down?
- Do true friends never hurt us?
- Are true friends those who help us the most?
- Why is it important to have lots of friends?
- Why is it important to have one true friend?
- Is it possible to have more than one true friend?
- Are there different types of friends?
- How many friends does one person need?
- What is the difference between a friend and a true friend?
- What qualities do you look for in a true friend?
- What is a best friend?
- What is the difference between a best friend and a true friend?
- Can friendship be unrequited?
- What if we didn't have friends?
- What if we didn't have true friends?
- What if everybody was friends?
- Can we be happy without friends?
- Can we choose our friends?
- Can a person live without friends?
- Would you let your parents or teachers choose your friends?
- Can you be 'just' friends with someone you are physically attracted to?
- Can you be friends with someone you have never met?
- How can online friends be real friends?
- When does friendship bring happiness?

- If you have no friends, is that the same as being lonely?

- How important is it that your friends are the same age as you?

- When could friends not be people?

- How do friends influence you?

- When do you know that you have a lifelong friend?

- What's the difference between a lifelong friend and a true friend?

- Is it ever okay to love your friends?

- If somebody always helps you, does that make them a friend?

- What is different about a friendship with your parents?

- When do your friends become like your extended family?

- Is it ever okay to be friends with your teacher?

- Are your siblings your friends?

- What is the difference between a friend and an enemy?

- What is the difference between a friend and a stranger?

- What do we call people who aren't our friends but who we know and who we don't dislike?

- Can friends be unkind and still be our friends?

- Who is most likely to be unkind, a friend or a stranger?

- Who is most likely to be a bully, a friend or a stranger?

- Do you always have to have shared interests with your friends?

# 3. CONSTRUCT UNDERSTANDING

## Activity 1: Diamond Ranking x2

In small groups ask your students to identify a set of qualities or characteristics that they value in a friend and agree on nine that they can use to rank in the structure below (Step 1).

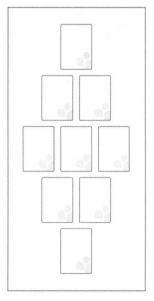

Students who require extra support can be provided with examples of characteristics to use during the Diamond Ranking exercise. See table below.

| trustworthy | fun | attractive |
| wise | kind | caring |
| loyal | a good listener | honest |
| interesting | fashionable | smart |
| plays sports | helpful | thoughtful |

Once your students have completed the Diamond Ranking (1), ask them to now re-rank the set of characteristics according to what they would value in a *true friend* (Step 2).

### Questions to Promote Further Dialogue

- What are the similarities and differences in the way we view friends and true friends?
- Which cards have remained in the same place and what does this show us about the different friendships?
- Which cards have been moved from the first Diamond Ranking and what are the reasons for this?

### Activity 2: Mystery

Introduce the following question:

**Was Toto Dorothy's only true friend?**

Give out the **Activity 2 resource cards** to your students. Working in pairs or small groups, they should read, sort and make sense of the information. Remind them that they will need to explain their thinking, conclusions and strategies to the rest of the group.

It is often useful to support the students when they are sorting through the information in front of them. This can help them to interpret and handle the information more easily and reconstruct their thinking to reach an understanding or conclusion.

| Evidence to show that Toto was Dorothy's only true friend. | Evidence to show that Toto was not Dorothy's only true friend. | Evidence that is not relevant. |
| --- | --- | --- |
|  |  |  |
| Our conclusion is . . . | | |
| The key reasons for this are . . . | | |

### Questions to Promote Further Dialogue

- What do we know about Dorothy? Can you describe her?
- How does Dorothy feel about each of her friends?

- How can we measure the friendship between Dorothy and the other characters?

- How does Dorothy know what a true friend is?

- Does Dorothy view Toto as a friend, a true friend or neither?

- How important is friendship to Dorothy?

- Who does Dorothy view as her true friend?

- How is Dorothy lonely?

- Is Dorothy loved?

- Is Toto good for Dorothy?

- Is Dorothy a good friend?

- Why were the characters from Oz friendly towards Dorothy?

- What do the Scarecrow's actions reveal about his friendship with Dorothy?

- Do Dorothy's friends influence her?

- Is it ever okay to let your friends influence you?

- Should Dorothy's true friend be the one who helps her the most?

- How was Dorothy a true friend to the other characters?

- Was Dorothy a selfish friend?

- Were the Scarecrow, the Tin Woodman and the Lion genuine friends?

- How did the Scarecrow, the Tin Woodman and the Lion benefit from their friendship with Dorothy?

- How does Dorothy feel about leaving her friends to return home?

- Friendship is one of the central themes of this text. What other themes can you identify?

## Adaptation

To simplify the activity, fewer cards could be presented or images could be used to deepen understanding. Audio or film extracts of the quotes could also be used. It is important to ensure that these match the exact quotes from the text to ensure accuracy.

## Extension

To extend the challenge, you could include a set of blank cards for students to add their own commentary or quotes. Encourage your students to find new evidence from the text to answer the key question. Your students could be asked to write up the results of the Mystery in essay form.

## 4. CONSIDER THE LEARNING JOURNEY

At the end of the activity it is usual to encourage your students to review their learning journey and the thinking process they have engaged in throughout the session.

This can include reflection on the thinking that has taken place to this point, and a summary and conclusion of the new understanding reached.

Explicit reference to Learning Intentions and Success Criteria is a good starting point for this reflection, but it is also helpful to return to and re-examine some key questions:

- What do the students understand about the concept of 'friendship'?

- What are the differences between a friend and a true friend?

- Can a person live without friends?

- Can we choose our friends?

- Are there different types of friends?

- When does friendship bring happiness?

- How have the students' views of the key characters changed or developed?

- How did the author's use of language enhance the students' understanding of the key characters, their intentions and the theme of friendship?

- What skills have the students used throughout the lesson?

- Where and when could they use the skills again in the future?

## Transfer Activities

Ask students to provide further examples of friendship. They can take inspiration from TV, books, film or politics. Challenge your students to identify the characteristics and qualities that these friends exhibited or that drew them together.

Examples might be:

Harry Potter, Ron Weasley and Hermione Granger

Joe Louis and Max Schmeling

John Adams and Thomas Jefferson

Mary Todd Lincoln and Elizabeth Keckley

John F. Kennedy and Frank Sinatra

Bob Hope and Dwight Eisenhower

Martina Navratilova and Chris Evert

Ronald Reagan and Margaret Thatcher

Ask your students to provide some personal and social skills guidance around the concept of 'friendship' that they could share with younger students in the school. This could be in the form of a presentation piece, a piece of writing or peer coaching.

# WWW•EBI

**WWW – What Worked Well . . .**

**EBI – Even Better If . . .**

# Which Is the Most Important Symbol in *The Great Gatsby*?

**KEY CONCEPT:** Symbolism

**KEY SKILLS:** Identifying the use of symbolism and imagery in a text
Citing textual evidence
Determining the figurative and connotative meanings of words
Analysing the development of themes or ideas in a text
Comparing and contrasting
Evaluating arguments

# Which Is the Most Important Symbol in *The Great Gatsby*?

## OVERVIEW:

This lesson will enhance your students' knowledge and understanding of the use and effects of symbolism in *The Great Gatsby*. It is important for your students to be familiar with the novel prior to this activity.

## KEY CONCEPT:

Symbolism

## KEY WORDS:

Symbolism, symbol, sign, character, mark, letter, hieroglyphic, ideogram, emblem, token, representation, figure, image, shape, badge, allegory and motif.

## LEARNING INTENTION:

To understand the importance of symbolism in *The Great Gatsby*.

## SUCCESS CRITERIA:

We can do the following:

- Identify and explore the connections between familiar symbols we may encounter in society today.

- Examine and discuss the key uses of symbolism in *The Great Gatsby*.

- Rank and judge the importance of key symbols in the text.

- Decide which is the most important symbol, using evidence from the text to justify our views.

## STRATEGIES USED:

Sorting and Classifying

Diamond Ranking

# 1. IDENTIFY IMPORTANT CONCEPTS

Some of the key areas to investigate within and around the concept of 'symbolism' are the following:

- Colour
- Motifs
- Metaphor
- Themes
- Allegory
- Wealth
- Poverty
- Aspirations
- The American Dream

# 2. CHALLENGE STUDENTS' UNDERSTANDING OF THE CONCEPT

Here are some examples of cognitive conflict we expect your students to experience:

| Opinion | Conflicting Opinion |
|---|---|
| Symbols are an effective way of communicating the meaning of something. | Symbols are not an effective way of communicating if everyone doesn't have a shared understanding of what they mean. |
| Symbols have universal meanings that everyone can understand. | Symbols shift their meanings depending on the context they are used in. For example, a chain can be symbolic of union or imprisonment. |
| Words are used to convey either symbolic or literal meaning. | Words can possess a symbolic meaning and a literal meaning simultaneously. For example, a pun or a euphemism can have both a literal and a symbolic meaning at the same time. |
| Symbolism enhances fiction for the reader by building richness and adding depth to the narrative. | Symbolism does not enhance fiction for the reader if they do not understand the symbolic nature of the text. |
| Symbolism relates to literature and is a device used by authors to enhance their writing. | Symbolism is an aspect of our everyday life and language usage. |

## Questions for Challenge

- What is symbolism?
- What makes something symbolic?
- What is a symbol?
- How do we know what a symbol is?
- Why do we use symbols?
- How do we use symbols?
- When do we use symbols?
- How do we rely on symbols?
- How reliable are symbols?
- What if there weren't symbols in our everyday life?
- Can we live without symbols?
- How important is symbolism as a literary device?
- How much is the symbolic meaning of something dependent upon individual perception?
- How much is the symbolic meaning of something dependent upon its context?
- Does everything have a symbolic meaning if we look hard enough for it?
- Is it possible to communicate without symbols?
- Is it possible for a symbol to have just one meaning?
- When does something or someone become symbolic?
- What makes symbols important?
- Who decides if something is a symbol?
- Why do we see symbols in areas such as advertising, literature and film?
- Why do writers use symbolism? How does it help their writing?
- What is the difference between a symbol and a metaphor?
- What is the difference between symbolism and imagery?
- What is the difference between a symbol and a motif?
- What is the difference between symbolism and allegory?

## Activity 1: Provoke the Discussion Through Sorting and Classifying

Get your students to work in groups of no more than four. Give each group a set of the **Activity 1 resource cards\***. Ask your students to sort the symbols or the symbolism represented on the cards into categories. They will need to decide upon the criteria for this.

Your students should be able to clearly identify what connects each of the cards in each of the sets they create. They should also be invited to allow the sets to become *Venn Diagram* in character if they find that there is the need for this.

Remember to stop the groups and ask them to compare their thinking, reasoning and organisation.

*It would be beneficial to add a selection of commercial symbols to this activity.

**Download the activity cards at**
**http://resources.corwin.com/**
**learningchallengelessons**

Image source:
dwleindecker/iStock.com

# 3. CONSTRUCT UNDERSTANDING

## Activity 2: Diamond Ranking

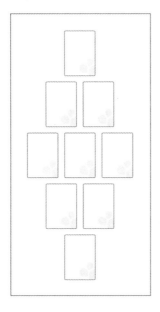

**online resources**

**Download the activity cards at** http://resources.corwin.com/ learningchallengelessons

LESSON 7
Which Is the Most Important Symbol in
*The Great Gatsby?*
2.1

**Daisy Buchanan**

She embodies the daisy flower, which is fragile but also grows wild. She is a fragile person who can't make up her own mind. The daisy has a golden yellow centre surrounded by white petals, symbolising her outward purity and innocence but morally corrupt core.

The Diamond Ranking strategy encourages active participation. It will help your students to prioritise information, clarify their thoughts and create reasons and reflections.

Using the **Activity 2 resource cards**, your students must choose nine of the symbols and/or examples of symbolism from *The Great Gatsby* and rank them according to their importance in the novel.

Your students can add their own examples of symbolism from the novel to the set to be ranked.

Encourage your students to move around the classroom to explore, discuss and challenge the ranking structures created by other groups.

## Questions to Promote Further Dialogue

- What makes one symbol more important than another?

- Which symbol aids the development of the plot most? Does this make it more important than other symbols?

- Should a key character be more important as a symbol than a setting, an action or an event?

- Should the most important symbol be the most powerful?

- Is the most frequently used symbol the same as the most important symbol?

- Does the number of connections a symbol has to characters, parts of the plot and settings increase its importance?

- Are the more complex examples of symbolism more important than the more simplistic and obvious examples?

- What is the link between the impact of the symbolism on the reader's enjoyment of the novel and its importance?

### Adaptation

Provide additional support for students by reading through the cards and defining difficult terms.

Limit the number of cards the students are interacting with in **Activity 1**.

Provide images for the symbols in **Activity 2**.

### Extension

Ask your students to find extra examples of symbols and symbolism in the novel in addition to those already provided.

Treat the activity title as an essay question and ask your students to create a response individually or in pairs. Use this as an opportunity for peer assessment and feedback.

# 4. CONSIDER THE LEARNING JOURNEY

At the end of the activity it is usual to encourage the students to review their learning journey and the thinking process they have engaged in throughout the session.

This can include reflection on the thinking that has taken place to this point and a summary and conclusion of the new understanding reached.

Explicit reference to Learning Intentions and Success Criteria is a good starting point for this reflection, but it is also helpful to return to and re-examine some key questions:

- Do you have a deeper or better understanding of the concept of 'symbolism'?
- Which parts of the lesson helped you to decide and/or change your knowledge and understanding of symbolism?
- What questions do you still have?
- What would you like to investigate further?
- Which is the most important symbol in *The Great Gatsby*?

### Ideas for Transfer

Ask your students to explore the use of symbolism in advertising and brands, exploring and identifying the most popular and the most important to us today.

Challenge your students to create a piece of descriptive writing around a chosen symbol. They could use ideas from *The Great Gatsby* such as lights and colours.

# WWW•EBI

# Which Example of Foreshadowing in *Of Mice and Men* Has the Most Impact on the Reader?

**KEY CONCEPT:** Foreshadowing

**KEY SKILLS:** Analysing the impact of word choice on the reader
Comparing and contrasting
Citing textual evidence
Demonstrating understanding of literary devices

# Which Example of Foreshadowing in *Of Mice and Men* Has the Most Impact on the Reader?

**OVERVIEW:**

The lesson will enhance your students' knowledge and understanding of the novella *Of Mice and Men*, focusing on John Steinbeck's use of foreshadowing. It is important for your students to be familiar with the novella prior to this activity.

**KEY CONCEPT:**

Foreshadowing

**KEY WORDS:**

Prediction, hints, clues, prognosticate, foreshow, foretell, indicate, suggest, signal, herald, augur, presage, portend, forewarn, prophecy, warn of, promise, impact and effect.

**LEARNING INTENTION:**

To understand the impact of foreshadowing in *Of Mice and Men*.

**SUCCESS CRITERIA:**

We can do the following:

- Identify examples of foreshadowing from the novella.

- Explain what foreshadowing is and how it is different from other literary devices and techniques.

- Discuss and explore the use and impact of foreshadowing on the reader.

- Interpret and evaluate the degree of impact caused by different examples of foreshadowing.

**STRATEGIES USED:**

Sorting and Classifying

Concept Line

# 1. IDENTIFY IMPORTANT CONCEPTS

Some of the key areas to investigate within and around the concept of 'foreshadowing' are the following:

- Direct and indirect foreshadowing
- Symbolism
- Literary devices
- Characterisation
- The American Dream
- The Wall Street Crash
- The Great Depression
- The working man
- The life and experiences of John Steinbeck

# 2. CHALLENGE STUDENTS' UNDERSTANDING OF THE CONCEPT

Here are some examples of cognitive conflict we expect your students to experience:

| Opinion | Conflicting Opinion |
|---|---|
| Foreshadowing enhances the reading experience by building dramatic tension and suspense. | Foreshadowing diminishes the reading experience by making the story predictable. For example: John Steinbeck makes it clear in the opening chapter of *Of Mice and Men* that Lennie can't survive the harsh realities of the Great Depression. |
| Foreshadowing places the reader at an advantage because they often know things before the characters in the text. | Foreshadowing places the reader at a disadvantage by causing confusion and misleading the reader with red herrings and false clues. |
| I need my teacher to tell me where foreshadowing is used as they have the expertise on literary techniques. The use of foreshadowing is primarily a literacy device specific to fictional literature. | I can work individually or on my own to identify examples of foreshadowing. Everyone can learn to do this. The use of foreshadowing is frequently used in a range of different media. For example: it is commonly used by composers of theatrical scores, in operas, film, television, gaming and spoken theatrical productions. |
| Foreshadowing is a technique that only experienced writers can use. | Foreshadowing is a technique that can be learnt and used by anyone. |

## Questions for Challenge

- What is foreshadowing?
- How do we identify foreshadowing?
- What are the differences between foreshadowing and other literary devices such as symbolism?
- What is the difference between foreshadowing and foreboding?

- What is the difference between foreshadowing and fate?
- What is the purpose of foreshadowing?
- What makes foreshadowing effective?
- How does foreshadowing enhance the experience for the reader?
- How does foreshadowing engage the reader more in the narrative?
- What would be the impact of not using foreshadowing at all?
- How is foreshadowing used as a plot device?
- How is foreshadowing used to create tension and suspense?
- Should we always use foreshadowing in our story writing?
- What if there was no such thing as foreshadowing?
- When should foreshadowing be used?
- When should foreshadowing not be used?
- When is foreshadowing effective in a narrative?
- Who should use foreshadowing in their writing?
- Can we write a successful narrative without using foreshadowing?
- How is foreshadowing used in other mediums, such as film?
- What is the difference in impact of using foreshadowing in films compared to literature?

# 3. CONSTRUCT UNDERSTANDING

**Download the activity cards at http://resources.corwin.com/ learningchallengelessons**

Image sources: Alphotographic/iStock.com (heron), DamianKuzdak/ iStock.com (rabbit)

## Activity 1: Provoke the Discussion Through Sorting and Classifying

Divide your class into small groups or pairs and distribute the **Activity 1 resource cards**, which contain quotations and images from the novella. Ask your students to sort and classify the quotations into the following two sets:

Set 1: Examples of foreshadowing

Set 2: Not examples of foreshadowing

Your students should discuss and share their criteria for sorting the cards and record this so that it can be shared with the whole group.

Your students will be using the foreshadowing resource cards they have selected for the Concept Line in the next activity.

## Activity 2: Concept Line

Your students should explore and analyse the examples of foreshadowing on the **Activity 1 resource cards**. Working in pairs or small groups, they should evaluate the degree of impact of each quotation upon the reader.

Create the Concept Line in your classroom as shown at the top of the next page and encourage your students to place the **Activity 1 resource cards** according to the significance of their impact. They should justify their decisions with reasons and constructively challenge and question each other's opinions.

## Questions to Promote Further Dialogue

- Why does Steinbeck use foreshadowing?

- When does Steinbeck use foreshadowing?

- Does foreshadowing have more impact if it appears earlier or later in the novella? Explain your reasons.

- How does Steinbeck use foreshadowing?

- What would the impact be if Steinbeck hadn't used foreshadowing?

- Why does foreshadowing have more impact if it centres around a key character like Lennie?

- How does the language used in foreshadowing affect the impact it has on the reader?

## Adaptation

Provide your students with fewer resource cards for each activity.

Provide additional support for students by reading through the cards and defining difficult terms.

## Extension

Your students could be challenged to find additional examples of foreshadowing from the novella that would help them to answer the key question.

Ask your students to write a mini essay, explaining and justifying how and why their chosen foreshadowing quotation has the most impact.

Ask your students to rank the examples of foreshadowing in the novella to establish which is the most important.

# 4. CONSIDER THE LEARNING JOURNEY

At the end of the activity it is usual to encourage the students to review their learning journey and the thinking process they have engaged in throughout the session.

This can include reflection on the thinking that has taken place to this point and a summary and conclusion of the new understanding reached.

Explicit reference to Learning Intentions and Success Criteria is a good starting point for this reflection, but it is also helpful to return to and re-examine some key questions:

- Do you have a deeper or better understanding of the concept of 'foreshadowing'?

- Which parts of the lesson helped you to decide and/or change your knowledge and understanding of foreshadowing?

Which Example of Foreshadowing in *Of Mice and Men* Has the Most Impact on the Reader?

Challenging LEARNING    103

- What questions do you still have?

- What would you like to investigate further?

- Which example of foreshadowing has the most impact on the reader? How do you know this?

### Ideas for Transfer

To develop your students' knowledge and understanding of John's Steinbeck's writing style and use of literary devices, ask your students to explore how foreshadowing is used in his other works, such as *The Grapes of Wrath*, *East of Eden* and *The Pearl*.

Ask your students to use foreshadowing in their own short story. They must first plan their short story and work out how they can use foreshadowing as a plot device. They could use similar ideas to *Of Mice and Men* by using setting at the start to foreshadow future events.

Show your students the film version of *Of Mice and Men* and ask them to discuss how they would use lighting, sound, editing and special effects to enhance the impact of foreshadowing.

# WWW•EBI

## WWW – What Worked Well . . .

## EBI – Even Better If . . .

LESSON

# 9

# Was It Acceptable for Liesel to Steal in *The Book Thief*?

**KEY CONCEPT:** Theft

**KEY SKILLS:** Crafting an argument

Evaluating arguments

Citing textual evidence

Analysing the development of a theme

Analysing a cultural experience as depicted in a text

Questioning

# Was It Acceptable for Liesel to Steal in *The Book Thief*?

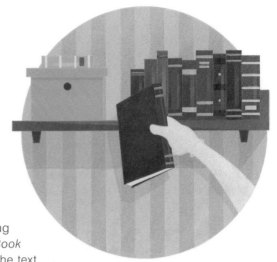

## OVERVIEW:

This lesson will enhance students' knowledge and understanding of the character Liesel and the morality of her actions in *The Book Thief*. It is important for students to have read and understood the text so they can access this lesson.

## KEY CONCEPT:

Theft

## KEY WORDS:

Theft, stealing, crime, wrongdoing, justifiable, dishonest, guilt, remorse, corruption, deceit, larceny, sinful, consequence and punishment.

## LEARNING INTENTION:

To be able to make an informed judgement on the uses of theft in *The Book Thief*.

## SUCCESS CRITERIA:

We can do the following:

- Describe what theft is and appreciate a range of ethical views regarding the issue.

- Discuss and explore the differing forms of theft to decide which are acceptable and which are unacceptable.

- Examine and determine whether theft can ever be justified.

- Identify and question Liesel's reasons for theft in *The Book Thief*.

- Evaluate the actions of Liesel to determine the morality of her actions.

- Determine whether the crimes Liesel committed were acceptable or not.

## STRATEGIES USED:

Concept Line

Opinion Line

Mystery

# 1. IDENTIFY IMPORTANT CONCEPTS

Some of the key areas to investigate within and around the concept of 'theft' are the following:

- The impact of theft upon victims
- The impact of theft on the economy
- Moral absolutism
- Moral relativism
- Historical attitudes towards theft
- International and cultural attitudes towards theft
- The law
- Religious views
- Different forms of theft
- Consequences of theft

# 2. CHALLENGE STUDENTS' UNDERSTANDING OF THE CONCEPT

Here are some examples of cognitive conflict we expect your students to experience:

| Opinion | Conflicting Opinion |
| --- | --- |
| Theft is always wrong. | Theft is sometimes justified. For example, it is not wrong to steal food to keep your children alive. |
| Stealing is acceptable if it helps others. For example, Robin Hood stole from the rich and gave to the poor. | Stealing is not acceptable in any circumstances. Robin Hood was an outlaw and had no right to take money that was not his. |
| Theft is only about stealing physical objects. | Theft takes many forms. For example, you can steal ideas, time, identity, innocence, etc. |
| Theft is a deliberate act of taking something that doesn't belong to you. | It is possible to accidentally take something that doesn't belong to you. For example, you could take the wrong school bag home. |
| Only bad people steal. | Most people in their lifetime will have stolen something. |

## Questions for Challenge

- What is a thief?
- What makes someone a thief?
- What is stealing?
- Why do people steal?
- What are the different reasons for people stealing?

- What if there was no such thing as stealing?
- Why do you think it is against the law to steal?
- Should we always obey the law?
- Is it possible to steal and not be a thief?
- Should we never steal?
- Should we never steal something that isn't ours?
- If you steal, should you always be punished?
- Who decides what a thief is?
- Can we steal without consequences?
- Is stealing always a deliberate act?
- What if we take items that don't belong to anyone? Is this still stealing?
- Are there things, beyond objects, that can be stolen?
- How is stealing wrong if it helps someone else?
- If you are poor and steal from someone rich, is that acceptable?
- Is it worse to steal someone's possessions or someone's ideas?
- What is the difference between copying and stealing?
- What is the difference between cheating and stealing?
- What is the difference between adults stealing from each other and children stealing from each other?
- Should we always forgive children who steal?
- Should we always forgive a person who steals for the first time?
- Should we steal if our needs are more important than others?
- Do some people have more right to steal than others?
- How does stealing make you a bad person?
- Should we judge an act of theft morally or criminally?
- If you say sorry for stealing, does that make it acceptable?
- Is stealing something valuable worse than stealing something of little or no value?
- How might we justify theft if it is for survival?
- When does stealing make the world more fair?
- When can your rights be stolen?
- If you have no shoes in winter, is it acceptable to steal them from a store?
- Is it better to steal from a store than from a person?
- Is it worse to steal from someone you know than from a stranger?
- If you borrow a jumper and forget to give it back, is that stealing?
- If we take something that used to belong to us, could this be called stealing?
- If a toddler eats bread from the store, is that stealing?
- If you take five minutes longer for your lunch break, is that stealing?
- If stealing can be justified as a necessary act, how should we view other criminal acts?

- When is stealing a necessary act?

- When is stealing morally right?

- When is stealing a selfish act?

- In times of natural disasters, is it acceptable to steal?

- Who decides when theft is acceptable?

# 3. CONSTRUCT UNDERSTANDING

## Activity 1: Concept Line

**Download the activity cards at**
http://resources.corwin.com/
learningchallengelessons

Distribute the **Activity 1/2 resource cards** to your students. They could work in pairs or small groups for this activity. Ask your students to read through each card and discuss how and if each scenario constitutes stealing.

Create the Concept Line in your classroom as shown below and ask your students to position each card according to how closely it corresponds to their understanding of stealing. Encourage your students to explain and justify the positioning of each card.

### Questions for Students

- What is stealing?

- How do we know what stealing is?

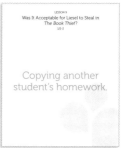

- What are the different types of stealing?

- Is stealing always a criminal act?

## Activity 2: Opinion Line

Encourage your students to engage in the moral dilemma of when and if stealing is ever acceptable. Using the **Activity 1/2 resource cards** again, ask your students to place each scenario on the Opinion Line based on how acceptable the 'stealing' is according to the views of their group. As with the previous activity, encourage your students to explain and justify the positioning of each card.

It would be beneficial for your students to share their Opinion Lines with other groups to compare and contrast their views on each scenario.

## Questions for Students

- Shouldn't all acts of theft be unacceptable?

- Which scenarios make theft more acceptable?

- Which scenarios were the easiest and most difficult to place? Why was this?

- How did these cards make you question your views on theft?

### Activity 3: Mystery

Divide the class into groups and distribute the **Activity 3 resource cards**. Students are to tackle a Mystery based upon the *The Book Thief*. Students are to use the Mystery to help them answer the following question:

**Was it acceptable for Liesel to steal?**

It is often useful to assist the students when they are sorting through the Mystery cards. This can help them interpret and handle the information more easily and reconstruct their thinking in order to reach an understanding.

**This Consider Chart can help them assimilate their thinking.**

| Evidence that supports the idea that it was acceptable for Liesel to steal. | Evidence that refutes the idea that it was acceptable for Liesel to steal. | Evidence that is not relevant. |
|---|---|---|
| | | |

Our conclusion is . . .

The key reasons for this are . . .

### Questions to Promote Further Dialogue

- What does Liesel steal?

- Why does Liesel steal?

- Who does she steal for?

- Do you agree or disagree with Liesel's actions? Explain your reasons for this view.

- Does Liesel steal or borrow? What are the differences between these two actions?

- Should we judge Liesel according to law or morality?

- Does Liesel feel guilty for her actions? How does this affect our view of her actions?

- How do other characters view her thefts? Do they think the thefts are acceptable?

- Should we view Liesel's actions differently because she is a child?

- How do we evaluate the morality of Liesel's actions if the laws of the country were unjust?

- How can we judge the morality of an individual in society if those in power are committing criminal acts?

- Should every individual, regardless of status or religion, be judged in the same way?

- If Hitler was stealing the educational opportunities of citizens by burning books, was it acceptable for Liesel to steal the books for her own development?

- Should we view the stealing of books in the same way as stealing food?

- Would we view Liesel's actions differently if she was in a more privileged position?

## Adaptation

For those who require more support, reduce the number of cards or resources they are categorising at any one time. For those who respond to greater visual stimulus, substitute a number of the cards for scenes from the 2013 film adaption.

## Extension

Your students could add to the statement cards in the Opinion Line activity. They could provide examples of when people steal and challenge their peers to decide whether this is acceptable or not.

Your students could create additional cards to be added to the Mystery activity.

Your students could be challenged to find evidence from the text to support or oppose the Mystery cards.

Your students could set up a mock courtroom and put Liesel on trial for stealing. Using the novel and their understanding of 1940s Germany, they could take on the role of prosecution and defence to decide whether it was acceptable for Liesel to steal.

Your students could use their Consider Charts as a writing frame for answering the following question:

**Was it acceptable for Liesel to steal?**

# 4. CONSIDER THE LEARNING JOURNEY

At the end of the activity it is usual to encourage the students to review their learning journey and the thinking progress they have engaged in throughout the session.

This can include reflection on the thinking that has taken place to this point and a summary and conclusion of the new understanding reached.

Explicit reference to Learning Intentions and Success Criteria is a good starting point for this reflection, but it is also helpful to return to and re-examine some key questions:

- What skills have you used throughout today's lesson?

- What do we know about stealing?

- Is stealing ever acceptable?

- Is it ever acceptable to break the law?

- Have you changed your mind about what stealing is and when it is acceptable?

- Has today's lesson challenged how you view Liesel and her actions?

- Was it acceptable for Liesel to steal considering her circumstances?

## Ideas for Transfer

Your students could explore what was considered to be criminal activity in previous centuries and the consequences that criminals faced for their actions.

Your students could explore what is considered to be criminal activity in different cultures and in different parts of the world.

Your students could produce a guide to help prevent their peers from falling victim to theft. This could be particularly relevant to those students going to college. They could pay particular attention to online theft and fraud.

Having explored this concept, you could ask your students to plan and write an essay in response to the key question.

Ask your students to watch the film version of the novel to determine if our view of her theft changes.

# WWW•EBI

EBI – Even Better If . . .

# Was Macbeth Really a Tragic Hero?

**KEY CONCEPT:** Tragic Hero

**KEY SKILLS:** Analysing character development

Analysing an author's word choice

Determining figurative and connotative meanings of words

Determining the use of literary devices

Analysing the effect of a text's structure and plot on the reader

Crafting an argument

# Was Macbeth Really a Tragic Hero?

## OVERVIEW:

This lesson will enhance students' knowledge and understanding of Macbeth and his potential role as a tragic hero. It is important for students to have a secure understanding of the play *Macbeth* so they can access this lesson.

## KEY CONCEPT:

Tragic hero

## KEY WORDS:

Ambition, war, hero, nobility, honour, loyalty, pride, fate, fatal flaw, tragedy, bravery, courage, sorrow, distress, suffering, downfall, defeat, justice, judgement, murder, innocence, villain, violence, cruelty, morality, sympathy, fear, pity, protagonist, antagonist, genre, anagnorisis, hubris, hamartia and catharsis.

## LEARNING INTENTION:

To understand if Macbeth's characteristics make him a tragic hero.

## SUCCESS CRITERIA:

We can do the following:

- Define the characteristics of a tragic hero.

- Discuss and explore our impressions of Macbeth.

- Explore key scenes within the play to identify features of Macbeth's behaviour and language.

- Evaluate the evidence to determine if Macbeth is a tragic hero.

## STRATEGIES USED:

Opinion Corners

Jigsaw Groups

Concept Target

# 1. IDENTIFY IMPORTANT CONCEPTS

Some of the key areas to investigate within and around the concept of 'tragic hero' are the following:

- Aristotle's view of a tragic hero
- Tragic flaws
- Conventions of a tragedy
- Fate vs. free will
- Tragic hero vs. villain
- Modern tragic hero

# 2. CHALLENGE STUDENTS' UNDERSTANDING OF THE CONCEPT

Here are some examples of cognitive conflict we expect your students to experience:

| Opinion | Conflicting Opinion |
|---|---|
| A tragic hero has a fatal flaw that causes their downfall. | It is a person's actions, not their flaws, that lead to their downfall. |
| A tragic hero deserves pity. | It is the victims, not the perpetrators, who deserve our pity. |
| A tragic hero is characterised by their flaws. | We all have flaws, but we are not all tragic heroes. |
| We identify with the struggles of a tragic hero. | Tragic heroes are privileged and powerful, so they are not like us at all. |
| Tragic heroes are fated to fail. | Tragic heroes create their own misery. |

## Questions for Students

- What is a tragic hero?
- What makes a tragic hero?
- How do we know what a tragic hero is?
- Should tragic heroes be strong?
- How do we relate to tragic heroes?
- Are tragic heroes important?
- Would you still be a tragic hero if you caused pain and suffering to others? Why?
- Should a tragic hero be the protagonist or the antagonist?
- What's the difference between a hero and a tragic hero?

- What makes a hero tragic?

- What's the difference between a tragic hero and a villain?

- Can a tragic hero also be a villain?

- What is a fatal flaw/tragic flaw?

- Doesn't everyone have flaws? What makes a flaw fatal?

- Should tragic heroes be blamed for their actions if they have a fatal flaw?

- Could anyone be a tragic hero?

- Do tragic heroes need to have been heroes first?

- Why would we feel pity for a tragic hero?

- Do tragic heroes deserve our pity?

- What do tragic heroes teach us?

- Are tragic heroes always male? Can you think of any female tragic heroes from literature, past or present?

# 3. CONSTRUCT UNDERSTANDING

**Activity 1: Opinion Corners**

Opinion Corners require students to make an exact choice. They are very useful for developing not only the skills of reasoning and explanation, but also the language of persuasion.

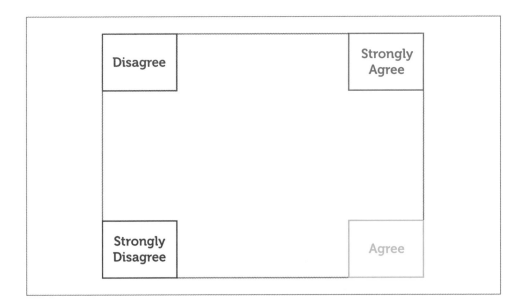

After you read each statement from the **Activity 1 resource cards**, your students should stand in the corner that best represents their opinion on the matter. Tell them they must choose one of the corners. They cannot stand somewhere in the middle. Once your students have chosen a corner, get them to talk about their choice with the people around them. After that, get a spokesperson from each corner to give a summary of the reasons why the people in their corner made the choice they did.

## Activity 2: Jigsaw Groups

Divide your students into seven groups. These are the home groups. Adjust the group size if the class size is smaller/larger than 24.

Give each home group access to a copy of the scene they will be studying (see below for list of scenes). The **Activity 2 resource cards** provide a summary of the key events from each scene. The scenes to be studied are:

- Act 1 Scene 2
- Act 1 Scene 3
- Act 1 Scene 4
- Act 1 Scene 5
- Act 1 Scene 7
- Act 2 Scene 1
- Act 2 Scene 2

Ask each home group to explore how Macbeth is presented in their scene, converting the statements from **Activity 1 resource cards** into questions:

- Is Macbeth a great man?
- Is Macbeth a hero?
- Can we relate to Macbeth's feelings/actions here?
- Is he a likeable character?
- Do we pity Macbeth?
- Are we afraid of Macbeth?
- Does Macbeth realise the consequences of his actions?

Encourage your students to record their discussions on a table like the one below. You can find a photocopiable example at the end of this lesson plan.

Not all the questions will be applicable to the scene studied. Students can complete the last column, which asks them to look for evidence elsewhere.

**Download the activity cards at http://resources.corwin.com/ learningchallengelessons**

| Act ... Scene ... | Yes (provide evidence) | No (provide evidence) | Maybe (provide evidence/ explanation) | Alternative evidence from another scene |
|---|---|---|---|---|
| Is Macbeth a great man? | | | | |
| Is Macbeth a hero? | | | | |

## Questions to Promote Further Dialogue

- Is Macbeth noble?

- Does Macbeth have 'great' qualities?

- Is Macbeth the protagonist or the antagonist?

- Is Macbeth a character we can relate to?

- Does Macbeth have a fatal flaw?

- What causes Macbeth's downfall?

- Why was Macbeth mentioned by the Witches at the very start of the play? Does this suggest he was doomed from the very start of the play?

- Was Macbeth controlled by his fatal flaw and/or fate? Or something/someone else?

- Why does Macbeth tell his wife, 'We shall proceed no further in this business?' and then kill King Duncan?

- Why does Macbeth kill King Duncan?

- Did Macbeth want to kill King Duncan?

- How does Macbeth react after killing King Duncan?

- Why does Macbeth kill Banquo and Macduff's family?

- Was Macbeth controlled by his ambition?

- Was Macbeth controlled by the Witches?

- Do we feel pity for Macbeth in the play?

- Could any other characters in the play be a tragic hero?

- When does Macbeth realise his mistakes?

- Can we feel pity for a man who murders innocent people?

- Does the audience learn from Macbeth's mistakes?

- If Macbeth isn't a tragic hero, what else could he be?

Once each home group feels they have a good understanding of how Macbeth is presented in their scene, they must share their understanding with the rest of the groups in the class.

Ask each student in the group to number themselves one to five. Now ask Person 1 from each group to sit together, and Person 2, etc. These new groups are the away groups. Each member of the away group takes it in turns to present their ideas about how Macbeth is presented in their scene. By sharing the information they have studied, the whole group gets a picture of Macbeth in the first section of the play.

Once all the information has been shared in the away group, the students can return to their home group and share what they have learned about the other segments.

### Activity 3: Concept Target

Ask your students to draw a Concept Target like the one shown below. In the inner circle they should write the following statement:

**Macbeth is a tragic hero.**

On small pieces of paper/card, your students should write all the ideas that relate to that concept or that have emerged through the dialogue process and the Jigsaw activity.

**Download the activity cards at http://resources.corwin.com/ learningchallengelessons**

LESSON 10
Was Macbeth Really a Tragic Hero?
3-4

'For brave Macbeth (well he deserves that name)

Disdaining fortune, with his brandish'd steel,

Which smoked with bloody execution.'

Sergeant

Alongside their ideas, students can also be given the **Activity 3 resource cards,** which contain a selection of quotations from the play.

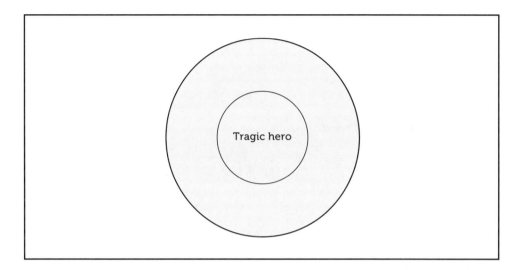

Students should take each idea or quotation in turn and decide whether it shows that Macbeth is **definitely** a tragic hero (in which case they should move it to the inner circle), **probably** a tragic hero (in which case they should put it in the outer circle) or **not** a tragic hero (in which case they should move it outside of the outer circle).

### Adaptation

Provide students with a timeline of key events in the play.

Ask students to answer a smaller selection of questions for the Jigsaw activity.

### Extension

Ask your students to create a timeline of Macbeth's actions to show his downfall. This would be a useful activity to identify the acts and scenes where Macbeth changes from a hero to a tragic hero. This activity could be turned into a Fortune Line with the x-axis being marked with each act in the play and the y-axis labelled from **hero** to **tragic hero**.

Having explored this concept, you could ask your students to plan and write an essay in response to the key question.

## 4. CONSIDER THE LEARNING JOURNEY

At the end of the activity it is usual to encourage your students to review their learning journey and the thinking process they have engaged in throughout the session.

This can include reflection on the thinking that has taken place to this point and a summary and conclusion of the new understanding reached.

Explicit reference to Learning Intentions and Success Criteria is a good starting point for this reflection, but it is also helpful to return to and re-examine some key questions:

- Has anyone changed their mind about what a tragic hero is?
- What do you know now that you didn't know before?

- Which idea really made you think?

- What skills have you used throughout the lesson?

- Is it important to agree on definitions together?

- What questions are you still thinking about?

## Ideas for Transfer

Use the questions from the Jigsaw activity to explore the following question:

**Is Lady Macbeth a tragic hero?**

Using a Venn Diagram, ask your students to compare Macbeth with other tragic characters in Shakespeare's plays, such as Othello, Hamlet or King Lear.

Challenge your students to write their own soliloquy for Macbeth that fits the characteristics for a tragic hero. Your students could decide when this soliloquy should be delivered.

Show your students two extracts from film versions of *Macbeth*. They can make notes on how his role as a tragic hero is presented. These notes could be transformed into a review or a critique of the two performances.

Examples of contexts where concept applies:

Examples of related ideas or associations:

Examples of phrases or sentences where concept is used:

Examples of wording or phrases of similar or opposite meaning:

# WWW•EBI

## EBI – Even Better If . . .

# Is Romeo Really In Love?

**KEY CONCEPT:** Love

**KEY SKILLS:** Analysing the development of a theme

Citing textual evidence

Drawing inferences

Determining the meaning of words or phrases used in a text

Analysing a cultural experience as depicted in literature

# Is Romeo Really In love?

## OVERVIEW:

This lesson has been produced to enhance your students' knowledge and understanding of how love is presented in the play, with particular focus on Romeo's words and behaviour. It is important for your students to be familiar with the plot and characters in *Romeo and Juliet* and to have some knowledge of when *Romeo and Juliet* was written and performed.

## KEY CONCEPT:

Love

## KEY WORDS:

Love, lust, maturity, passion, experience, maturity, immaturity, commitment and relationships.

## LEARNING INTENTION:

To understand how love is presented in *Romeo and Juliet*.

## SUCCESS CRITERIA:

We can do the following:

- Consider and question our own understanding of love.

- Enquire into different types of love.

- Challenge our own and other's opinions of love.

- Critically consider Romeo's language and behaviour to determine if he is really in love.

## STRATEGIES USED:

Mystery

Opinion Line

# 1. IDENTIFY IMPORTANT CONCEPTS

Some of the key areas to investigate within and around the concept of 'love' are the following:

- The definition of love
- The different types of love
- Love at first sight
- Attitudes to love in the Elizabethan era
- Age and maturity
- Forbidden love
- Subconscious love
- Predisposition to being in love

# 2. CHALLENGE STUDENTS' UNDERSTANDING OF THE CONCEPT

Here are some examples of cognitive conflict we expect your students to experience:

| Opinion | Conflicting opinion |
|---|---|
| Love makes us feel valued. | Unrequited love makes us feel worthless. |
| Love is romantic. | The love I have for my pets is not romantic. |
| It is always nice to be loved. | There are some people whose love we don't want. |
| Love is impossible to define. | Everyone knows what love is. |
| Love cannot be measured. | Love is a measure of how much we value something. |
| Love should be unconditional. | Love is dependent upon feelings, circumstance, reciprocation, etc. |

## Questions for Challenge

- What is love?
- How do we know what love is?
- How do we know when we, or someone else, is in love?
- How might you behave differently if you were in love?
- Should we always look for love?
- What makes someone fall in love?
- What if there was no such thing as love?
- Is it possible to be in love with more than one person?
- Who decides if you are in love?

- Can we live without love?

- Why do we say that people 'fall' in love?

- What's the difference between love and lust?

- What are the different types of love and do they all have the same value/importance?

- Do you need to have experience of love to know love?

- Do you need to be an adult to know/to be in love?

- Can we choose with whom we fall in love?

- If you marry someone, does it always mean you love them?

- Are some people more predisposed to falling in love than others?

- Is there a difference between 'young love' and 'older love'?

- Is there such thing as 'love at first sight'?

- Is love different for men than it is for women?

- Do we choose to be in love or is it something that happens to us?

# 3. CONSTRUCT UNDERSTANDING

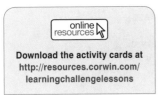

**Download the activity cards at http://resources.corwin.com/learningchallengelessons**

LESSON 11
Is Romeo Really In Love?
1-1

Love is important.

LESSON 11
Is Romeo Really In Love?
1-2

Love at first sight is just the same as lust at first sight.

### Activity 1: Opinion Line

Your students should use an Opinion Line to explore the statements found on the Activity Cards. There are two sets of cards: an orange set and a blue set. The blue cards offer an additional element of challenge.

Students should consider the statements and decide where they would position themselves on the line:

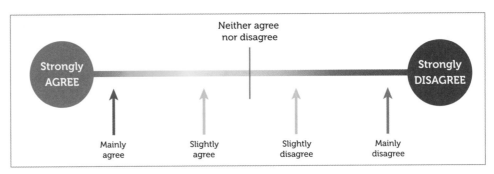

Ask students to persuade the person next to them of their opinion. The teacher can direct questions at individuals or groups that have clustered to explore their thinking.

Example questions to challenge students' thinking when using the Opinion Line:

- What do we mean by adult? (Age, maturity, responsibility, age of consent, voting?)

- Is 'understand' the same as 'feel'?

- What is true love?

- Can love exist if it isn't true?

- How can you decide if a person is in love? Is love something you can measure?

## Activity 2: Mystery

A Mystery is a useful tool for challenging the thinking of students.

Introduce the following question:

**Is Romeo in love?**

Give out **Activity 2 resource cards**. In pairs or small groups, encourage your students to sort the cards according to their own criteria.

It is useful to support your students when they are sorting through the information in front of them. This can help them to interpret and handle the information more easily and to reconstruct their thinking in order to reach an understanding.

A Consider Chart can be used in the classroom to help your students reflect on the dialogues they have had about Romeo and to encourage them to think about their perspective on love.

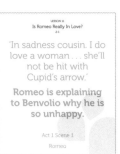

LESSON 11
Is Romeo Really In Love?
2-1

'In sadness cousin. I do love a woman . . . she'll not be hit with Cupid's arrow.'

Romeo is explaining to Benvolio why he is so unhappy.

Act 1 Scene 1
Romeo

| Evidence to show that Romeo is in love. | Evidence to show that Romeo isn't in love. | Evidence that is not relevant. |
|---|---|---|
|  |  |  |

Our conclusion is . . .

The key reasons for this are . . .

## Sorting and Classifying

- What do we know about Romeo? (Assess prior knowledge.)

- How does he view love?

- Does Romeo understand what love is? Does anyone?

- Does Friar Lawrence believe that Romeo is in love?

- Does Romeo behave differently with Juliet compared to Rosaline?

- Is it possible to fall in love with someone you have only just met?

- Why did Romeo want to get married so quickly? Does this prove he is in love?

- Is Paris in love with Juliet?

- Do Romeo and Paris view love in similar or different ways?

- Does love always mean sacrificing everything for another person? (Even your own life?)

- Would people have viewed love differently in the Elizabethan era compared to now or is the concept of 'love' universal and timeless?

### Adaptation

Cards can be simplified with an added translation of the quotation.

An image to enhance understanding of the language: Cupid, thorn, lips, love's heavy burden.

An image of the person who is speaking to distinguish between Friar Lawrence, Romeo, Juliet and Paris.

### Extension

To add extra challenge to **Activity 2**, your students could make their own Mystery cards. They can find and add extra ideas/quotations from the play. Alternatively, give students a smaller selection of the Mystery cards so that they need to find more of the evidence themselves.

Ask your students to put the cards in a time line to identify if Romeo's language or views on love change over time.

Ask your students to compare the language and behaviour of Paris and Romeo to determine how they view love. Students could use a Venn Diagram to record their ideas.

Having explored this concept, you could ask your students to plan and write an essay in response to the key question.

## 4. CONSIDER THE LEARNING JOURNEY

At the end of the activity it is worthwhile to encourage the students to review their learning journey and the thinking process they have participated in throughout the lesson.

This can consist of reflection on the thinking that has taken place by summarising and concluding on their new-found understanding.

Explicit reference to Learning Intentions and Success Criteria is a good starting point for this reflection, but it is also helpful to consider some of the following questions:

- Do you have a deeper understanding of the concept of 'love'?

- What conclusions have you drawn in this lesson about the concept that you could explain to someone else?

- What will you take away from this lesson that you'll remember?

- Do you have an understanding of this concept that will be useful in relation to further study of this book and period in history?

- Do you feel differently about your position on the Opinion Line? If you would want to change your opinion, could you explain why?

- You could recreate the Opinion Line here if time allows.

## Ideas for Transfer

Ask your students to carry out further research on the Elizabethan era and their typical definitions of love. They could use a Venn Diagram to identify the similarities and differences between then and now.

Encourage your students to explore how love is presented in a range of love poems. There are some possible options below. Allocate one poem per group for students to explore. Once each poem has been explored, each group could split up and find another poem to compare theirs to. Each student should attempt to explain their poem and then together they can create a Venn Diagram to compare the representation of love.

Ask your students to write a diary entry for Romeo using extracts and evidence from the play.

Show your students both modern and more traditional versions of the play, asking them to explore and discuss how they represent love. They could focus on features such as music, lighting and camera angles.

### 'She Walks in Beauty'

Lord Byron (1788–1824)

### 'Valentine'

Carol Ann Duffy (1955–)

### 'I Wanna Be Yours'

John Cooper Clarke (1949–)

### 'Sonnet 116'

Shakespeare (1564–1616)

### 'Love After Love'

Derek Walcott (1930–2017)

# WWW•EBI

EBI – Even Better If . . .

# Who Has the Most Power in *Romeo and Juliet?*

**KEY CONCEPT:** Power

**KEY SKILLS:** Analysing the development of a theme

Analysing an author's word choice

Citing textual evidence

Drawing inferences

Determining the meaning of words or phrases used in a text

Analysing a cultural experience as depicted in literature

# Who Has the Most Power in *Romeo and Juliet?*

## OVERVIEW

This lesson will enhance students' knowledge and understanding of the play *Romeo and Juliet* by William Shakespeare, focusing on the role of power as a theme within the work. It is important for students to be familiar with the play prior to this activity.

## KEY CONCEPT:

Power

## KEY WORDS:

Power, gender, wealth, violence, beauty, religion, the monarchy, control, strength, influence, authority, rule, command, dominance and the law.

## LEARNING INTENTION:

To understand the role and influence of power in the play *Romeo and Juliet*.

## SUCCESS CRITERIA:

We can do the following:

- Create a definition of power through enquiry of the concept.

- Discuss and explore the different types of power held by individuals in the play.

- Assess the way in which language conveys the power of a character.

- Rank the level of power each character holds, using evidence and events to justify our views.

## STRATEGIES USED:

Diamond Ranking

Concept Line

# 1. IDENTIFY IMPORTANT CONCEPTS

Some of the key areas to investigate within and around the concept of 'power' are the following:

- Wealth and power
- Gender and power
- Religion and power
- Violence and power
- Love and power
- Law and power
- Monarchy and power
- Relationships and power
- Types of power
- Symbols of power
- Exercise of power
- Soft vs. hard power

# 2. CHALLENGE CONCEPTUAL UNDERSTANDING

Here are some examples of cognitive conflict we expect your students to experience:

| Opinion | Conflicting Opinion |
|---|---|
| Power and authority go together. One always leads to the other. | A person can possess authority but not power. For example, Queen Elizabeth II has authority as the reigning monarch of the United Kingdom but no real power to exert her own will over the people. |
| Ruling governments are the most powerful and influential people in a country. | Governments can be influenced by citizens exercising their power over their leaders through mass protests and demonstrations. |
| The pursuit of power and influence leads to exploitation, violence and abuse. For example, Adolf Hitler rose to become one of the most powerful and destructive dictators in modern history. | The pursuit of power can have a positive impact. For example, Martin Luther King Jr. commanded powerful movements that affected positive change without military force and inspired social reform through non-violent protests. |
| Money is power because it allows you to buy more power and influence over others. | Real power cannot be bought; it is achieved by hard work and earned with respect. |
| The power of the mind can have a huge, positive impact on our ability to achieve something. | The power of the mind can have a huge, negative impact on our ability to achieve something. |

## Questions for Challenge

- What is power?

- What makes someone powerful?

- How do we know what power is?

- How do we know if someone has power?

- What does power look like?

- What does the absence of power look like?

- Is power something we can measure?

- Is power something we can see?

- Is power something we can feel?

- How do people gain power?

- Can you be born with power?

- Does everyone have power?

- Can we decide on how much power we have?

- Are there different types of power?

- Can someone have power because of their appearance?

- How else do people demonstrate their power?

- Do you need money to have power?

- Is it possible to be powerful and penniless?

- Does money always make you more powerful?

- Does being in love make you powerful?

- Is violence more powerful than love?

- Is power fair?

- Can a child have power?

- What if we have power and we don't want it? Can we give it away?

- Can power be taken away? Is this possible?

- What if everybody had power?

- Is it possible to be powerful and powerless at the same time?

- Are older people always more powerful than younger people?

- Who has the most power over us? Friends or family?

- What is the difference between power and control?

- What is the difference between having power and being powerful?

- What is the difference between power and influence?

- Does power always lead to authority?

- Does the law always have complete power over everyone?

- Do men have more power than women?

- Are strong people more powerful?

- Are happy people more powerful?

- What strategies or skills are needed to become more powerful?

- Is power permanent?

- Is there a supreme power? What is this?

- What is the difference between power and influence?
- Do job titles give someone power?
- Does a group of people always have more power than an individual?
- Should power be held by the most important people?
- Why is power desirable to people?
- Is the pursuit of power a basic human motive?
- Should we all aspire to have power?
- What is the difference between political and social power?
- What does 'knowledge is power' mean?
- Can the past have more power than the present?
- How does language reflect power?
- Do words have power? Can words have more power than an action?
- Can a person have power without words/language?
- Who has the most power in this classroom? How do you know this?

# 3. CONSTRUCT UNDERSTANDING

## Activity 1: Diamond Ranking

The Diamond Ranking strategy encourages active participation. It will help your students to prioritise information, clarify their thoughts and create reasons and reflections.

Students should now work individually or in groups to answer the following question:

**Who has the most power in *Romeo and Juliet*?**

They must rank the characters from *Romeo and Juliet* based on how much power they hold.

The **Activity 1 resource cards** can be found online. The teacher or your students can choose the nine characters to be ranked from the set.

**Download the activity cards at http://resources.corwin.com/ learningchallengelessons**

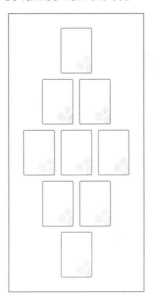

## Questions to Promote Further Dialogue

- Who has the most power in the play? How do you know this?

- Who has the least power in the play? How do you know this?

- How can we measure a character's power in the play?

- Who has the most lines in the play? Does this tell us their level of power?

- What do we know about Elizabethan times that would help our understanding of how power was distributed throughout society at that time?

- What do we know about women's rights at this time? Does Juliet have any power considering her future husband is decided by her father?

- Can an attitude be more powerful than a person?

- Who does Shakespeare give the most power to?

- Which character has the most power over other people?

- What are the different types of power shown in the play?

- Are the important characters in the play always the most powerful? The Prince has an important role, so does he have more power than the other characters, despite the fact that he can't stop the fighting/stop the deaths of Romeo and Juliet?

- Do the older characters have more power than the younger characters? Does Lord Montague have more power than Romeo?

- Do individual characters have more power than groups? Does Tybalt have more power than the Capulet household?

- Does the past 'ancient feud' hold more power than the present actions of the characters?

- How much power does Tybalt hold over the characters?

- Who has power over Tybalt?

- How much power do the servants have at the start of the play?

- Do any of the characters lose power? If so, how and why do they lose this power?

- How powerful is religion in the play? What would have happened if Romeo and Juliet couldn't have married?

- Who else knew about the marriage between Romeo and Juliet? Did they hold power because of knowledge?

- Does the Nurse have power over Juliet?

**Download the activity cards at http://resources.corwin.com/ learningchallengelessons**

LESSON 12
Who Has the Most Power in Romeo and Juliet?
2-2

'Then hie you hence to Friar Lawrence's cell. There stays a husband to make you a wife.'

Act 2 Scene 5

## Activity 2: Concept Line

Ask your students to look at the list of characters found in the **Activity 2 resource cards**. For each of the characters in this resource set, the students are provided with a key quotation along with an explanation of that quote.

In contrast to the previous Ranking activity (**Activity 1**), explain to your students that for this activity, they need to consider the amount of individual power being conveyed in the language used by the characters.

Specifically, and solely based on the language used, ask your students to place the characters along the line, in order of power, from least to most powerful.

You could also encourage students to find their own quotations that may offer a different interpretation of the character and their power.

The characters should be placed above the line and the quotation below the line.

Encourage discussion of the language used by the characters. How does the character's use of language determine their level of power?

## Adaptation

Provide a brief explanation about each character on the cards used in **Activity 2**, e.g. 'age', 'daughter of', 'picture'.

You could select a smaller range of cards.

## Extension

Students could select their own characters and quotations for the Concept Line.

Diamond Ranking activity – who would have the most power in today's world?

Ask students to consider how/if the characters would be ranked differently if the play was written today. You could identify nine characters for your students from the **Activity 1 resource cards** or leave the choice to them.

Fortune Line – to track the power held by specific characters through the play, students could choose a character and create a Fortune Line.

On the horizontal axis, students position the key stages from the play (or beginning, middle and end) and on the vertical axis they measure the power at each stage.

- The students could identify key stages from a scene, from an act or from the whole play. This would encourage students to explore the development of character and theme. An example of how this activity could work with a scene would be tracking Juliet's power in Act 3 Scene 5.
- Challenge students to identify changes in the language used by the characters.
- Challenge students to explore why this power changes, or why it stays constant.

Having explored this concept, you could ask your students to plan and write an essay in response to the key question.

# 4. CONSIDER THE LEARNING JOURNEY

At the end of the activity it is usual to encourage your students to review their learning journey and the thinking process they have engaged in throughout the session.

This can include reflection on the thinking that has taken place to this point and a summary and conclusion of the new understanding reached.

Explicit reference to Learning Intentions and Success Criteria is a good starting point for this reflection, but it is also helpful to return to and re-examine some key questions:

- What makes someone powerful?
- How do we know if someone has power?
- What does power look like?
- Are there different types of power?
- Does being in love make you powerful?
- What's the difference between power and control?
- How does language reflect power?

To encourage the students to further review their learning journey and their thinking progress, students could provide a case and reasoning for the following key question:

**Who has the most power in *Romeo and Juliet*?**

Each student or group chooses who they believe holds the most power and presents an argument to the rest of the class on their choice. They could be asked to support their argument with three key reasons that can be supported by specific quotations from the text. The other groups could have opportunities to question the reasoning given.

## Ideas for Transfer

Ask your students to identify the nine most significant people alive in the world today. Then ask them to rank these people according to their power. This could become a visual display with information about each person focusing on the power that they hold.

Alternatively, your students could explore and rank the power held by: the government, the police, school, family, the weather, the monarchy, science, the media, social media, the medical profession and art (substitute and change according to the needs of your class).

Assign a character from the **Activity 1 resource cards** and ask your students to provide notes on how that character should exhibit power in their performance.

Encourage your students to investigate the local media to determine who has the most power, exploring news channels and social networking sites.

# WWW•EBI

**WWW – What Worked Well . . .**

**EBI – Even Better If . . .**

# Is Tybalt a Villain or a Victim?

**KEY CONCEPTS:** Victim, Villain

**KEY SKILLS:** Analysing character development

Analysing an author's word choice

Citing textual evidence

Crafting an argument

Analysing the treatment of a theme across multiple texts

# Is Tybalt a Villain or a Victim?

## OVERVIEW:

This lesson will enhance students' knowledge and understanding of the play *Romeo and Juliet* by William Shakespeare, focusing on the characterisation and role of Tybalt. It is important for students to have read and understood the events of the play so they can access this lesson.

## KEY CONCEPTS:

Victim

Villain

## KEY WORDS:

Violence, patriarchy, tradition, loyalty, honour, characterisation, fear, dominance, villainous, felon, outlaw, innocent, control, hate and love.

## LEARNING INTENTION:

To understand the characterisation of Tybalt as a villain and/or victim in *Romeo and Juliet*.

## SUCCESS CRITERIA:

We can do the following:

- Discuss and explore what we understand by the terms 'victim' and 'villain'.
- Identify typical villains and victims in literature and film.
- Explore and analyse the language used by Tybalt and other characters in *Romeo and Juliet*.
- Apply our understanding of the terms 'victim' and 'villain' to the characterisation of Tybalt.
- Determine Tybalt's role in the play.

## STRATEGIES USED:

Mystery

Venn Diagram

Opinion Line

# 1. IDENTIFY IMPORTANT CONCEPTS

Some of the key areas to investigate within and around the concepts of 'victim' and 'villain' are the following:

- Crime

- Innocence

- Violence

- Evil

- Power

- Weakness

- Cause and effect

- Misfortune

- Revenge

- Hierarchy

- Family honour

- Patriarchal society

## Activity 1: Provoke the Discussion Using a Diagram

Divide your students into small groups and distribute the **Activity 1 Orange resource cards.**

Ask the students to sort through the cards according to whether they classify each character as a villain or a victim. This activity should help the students develop their understanding of the concepts.

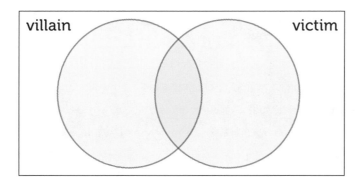

Download the activity cards at http://resources.corwin.com/learningchallengelessons

## Questions for Students

- What is a villain/victim?

- What is it that makes someone/something a villain/victim?

- What are the main differences between a villain and a victim?

- Can you identify any more victims and villains from the books and films you have read and watched? How do these fit into your categories?

- Have you identified any characters who are both villain and victim?

The **Activity 1 Orange resource cards** contain a range of characters from literature/ films. Depending on the age and reading habits of your students, it may be more useful to select the more familiar names and ask the groups to think of their own examples of villains and victims from the literature they read at home or at school.

The **Activity 1 Blue resource cards** containing villains and victims from other Shakespeare plays should be used for those who have a wider knowledge and understanding of other plays. There are also opportunities here to encourage students to add their own examples from the plays/novels they have studied.

# 2. CHALLENGE STUDENTS' UNDERSTANDING OF THE CONCEPT

Here are some examples of cognitive conflict we expect your students to experience:

| Opinion | Conflicting Opinion |
|---|---|
| Villains are social misfits and outcasts. | Some villains, such as Gaston in *Beauty and the Beast*, are popular and socially revered. |
| Villains are hated characters. | Villains make stories more interesting. |
| Victims are powerless and weak like Tiny Tim. | Victims can be strong and resilient like Oliver Twist. |
| Villains have no conscience. | Ebenezer Scrooge was a villain whose conscience changed his behaviour. |
| A person who has been hurt by someone else is a victim. | A strong tackle in a team game may hurt but it doesn't make me a victim. |
| You can choose whether to be a victim or not. | Nobody would choose the events that make them a victim. |

## Questions for Challenge

- What makes someone a victim/villain?
- How do we know if someone/something is a villain or a victim?
- Who decides what a villain/victim is?
- Would you be a villain if you were despised by others?
- Would you always be a victim if people felt sorry for you?
- Are people ever destined, at birth, to become a victim/villain?
- Are villains always inherently evil?
- Can we choose to be a villain/victim or is it decided by others?
- Are villains always the 'bad guys'? Can you think of any examples that confirm or contradict this idea?
- Should we always fear villains?
- Can a villain have morals?
- Are villains always the opposite of victims?
- Do villains always hold power?

- Are victims always powerless?

- Are victims always innocent?

- Is there a 'typical' villain/victim?

- How are victims and villains similar/different in their characteristics and attributes?

- What is the difference between a victim's and a villain's judgement of what villainous behaviour is?

- Is it possible to be a villain and a victim at the same time?

- Can victims become villains because of how they have been treated?

- To what extent are villains a victim of their own flaws?

- If you commit a villainous act, does this always make you a villain?

- Is it ever possible to be a victim or a villain and not know it?

- What is the difference between a criminal and a villain?

- What is the difference between an antagonist and a villain?

# 3. CONSTRUCT UNDERSTANDING

### Activity 2: Mystery

A Mystery is a useful tool for challenging the thinking of your students. In groups of two or three, present your students with the **Activity 2 resource cards**. Then ask your students to use and assess this evidence as a way to answer the following question:

**Is Tybalt a villain or a victim?**

It is often useful to support the students when they are sorting through the information in front of them. This can help them interpret and handle the information more easily and reconstruct their thinking to reach an understanding. In the table below, students can record their ideas on the evidence that shows whether Tybalt is a victim or a villain.

Challenge the students to find evidence that isn't included in the Mystery activity by allocating key scenes to each group: Act 1 Scene 1, Act 1 Scene 5 and Act 3 Scene 1.

online resources

**Download the activity cards at http://resources.corwin.com/learningchallengelessons**

LESSON 13
Is Tybalt a Villain or a Victim?
2-1

'Romeo slew Tybalt;
Romeo must not live!'

**Lady Capulet wants to avenge the death of Tybalt and demands that Romeo should lose his life.**

Act 3 Scene 1

Lady Capulet

LESSON 13
Is Tybalt a Villain or a Victim?
2-2

'O courteous Tybalt, honest gentleman,

That ever I should live to see thee dead.'

**The nurse grieves over the death of Tybalt.**

Act 3 Scene 2

Nurse

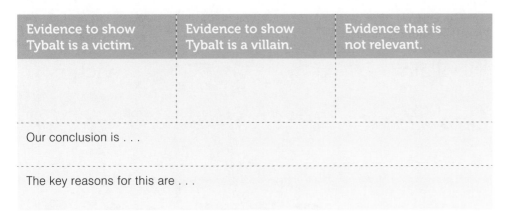

| Evidence to show Tybalt is a victim. | Evidence to show Tybalt is a villain. | Evidence that is not relevant. |
|---|---|---|
| | | |

Our conclusion is . . .

The key reasons for this are . . .

A more creative and visual way to present the surroundings could be an image of Tybalt's face/outline that is split into two sections. Students present villain and victim evidence in each half with the irrelevant information outside the outline.

## Questions to Promote Further Dialogue

- What do we know about Tybalt? (Assess prior knowledge.)
- How is he similar/different from the other characters in Act 1 Scene 1?
- What makes Tybalt a villain/victim or both?
- Do the other characters view Tybalt as a victim or a villain?
- Do you agree with the views of the other characters?
- Does Shakespeare present Tybalt as a victim or a villain? How do you know this?
- Did Tybalt always have wicked intentions? What was his motivation for wanting to kill Romeo?
- Does Tybalt's anger make him more of a villain?
- Are Romeo and Tybalt both villains for committing murder?
- When Tybalt is killed by Romeo, does he become a victim?
- Could Tybalt be a victim of a patriarchal society?
- Is Tybalt wholly responsible for the fighting between the two families?
- Did Tybalt want to kill Mercutio?
- If Tybalt isn't a villain, then who is?
- If Tybalt isn't a victim, then who is?
- Is it fair to view Tybalt as a villain when many of the characters are involved in the fighting?
- If Tybalt is viewed as a villain, should we label Mercutio a villain as well?
- Is Tybalt responsible for the feud between the two families?
- Do we ever feel sympathy for Tybalt? Does this affect our view of him?

### Activity 3: Venn Diagram

To explore the concepts further, students could investigate the possibility of Tybalt being both a villain and a victim. Using the information from **Activity 2**, students work in pairs to sort the evidence from the Mystery activity into the Venn Diagram according to the following question:

**Tybalt – villain or victim?**

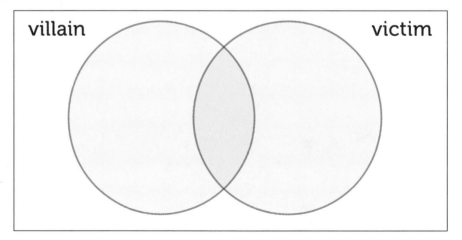

Your students could then work in pairs to explore the rest of the play, adding evidence and ideas to the relevant circle.

## Adaptation

The teacher selects a smaller range of cards for the Mystery.

## Extension

To add more challenge for both activities, give your students fewer cards so they can explore and investigate their own villains and victims and their own evidence from the play.

Ask students to create a list of the features we would expect to find in a villain and a victim based on their investigations from this lesson.

Having explored this concept, you could ask your students to plan and write an essay in response to the key question.

# 4. CONSIDER THE LEARNING JOURNEY

At the end of the activity it is usual to encourage your students to review their learning journey and the thinking process they have engaged in throughout the session.

This can include reflection on the thinking that has taken place to this point and a summary and conclusion of the new understanding reached.

The teacher could introduce an Opinion Line where students position themselves on the line, explaining their reasons using evidence from the text.

Use 'Tybalt is a villain' followed by 'Tybalt is a victim'.

It will be interesting to highlight the contrast between the two positions your students take up. For some students, this might mean that they do not actually move at all.

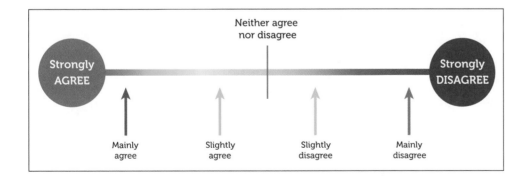

Ask your students to sum up in one sentence their thoughts on 'Is Tybalt a victim or a villain?' This sentence can be supported by three key reasons in order to evaluate and concentrate their thinking.

Possible questions to review the learning journey are:

- Has anyone changed their mind about what a villain and a victim is?

- What do you know now that you didn't know before?

- Which idea really made you think?

- What skills have you used throughout the lesson?

- Is it important to agree on definitions together?

- What questions are you still thinking about?

## Ideas for Transfer

Depending on the students' knowledge of other Shakespeare plays, the students could compare the villains from different texts, for example a Venn Diagram with two/three circles with Macbeth, Tybalt and Regan. Alternatively, use three villains from Shakespeare plays to identify the Odd One Out, which should provoke discussion on the similar and different traits of villainous characters.

Encourage students to research and explore villains from a wider range of media or literature. Students could create a montage of images representing the terms 'villain' and 'victim'.

Ask your students to investigate Carl Jung's archetypal figures to gain a deeper understanding of universal character types.

Ask your students to create their own characters to typify/challenge the villain and victim roles. These could be characters for a chosen Marvel comic or a genre of their choice. Alternatively, you could allocate a character to each pair/group and ask students to transform that character into a victim or a villain, for example: transform Cinderella into a villain.

# WWW•EBI

| WWW – What Worked Well . . . |
| --- |
| |

| EBI – Even Better If . . . |
| --- |
| |

# Is Fame Important?

**KEY CONCEPT:** Fame

**KEY SKILLS:** Analysing the use of language in poetry

Determining an author's point of view

Citing textual evidence

# Is Fame Important?

## OVERVIEW:

This lesson will enhance students' knowledge and understanding of Emily Dickinson's life, letters and poetry to determine her views on fame. It would be beneficial for your students to have some understanding of poetry terminology prior to this lesson.

## KEY CONCEPT:

Fame

## KEY WORDS:

Fame, celebrity, popularity, glory, greatness, recognition, stardom, prestige, reputation, renown, rank, status, acclaim, accolade, admiration, visibility, importance and privacy.

## LEARNING INTENTION:

To understand Emily Dickinson's views on fame.

## SUCCESS CRITERIA:

We can do the following:

- Explore and define what fame means to us.

- Discuss and question the importance of fame in society.

- Investigate the life of Emily Dickinson to consider her views and ideas on fame.

- Analyse the poetry of Emily Dickinson to evaluate how fame is presented.

## STRATEGIES USED

Ranking

Venn Diagram

Opinion Line

# 1. IDENTIFY IMPORTANT CONCEPTS

Some of the key areas to investigate within and around the concept of 'fame' are the following:

- Celebrity culture
- Stardom
- Freedom
- Social media and networking
- Private vs. public
- Fame and infamy
- Ambition
- Anonymity
- Loneliness
- Reality
- Power
- The traditional roles and expectations of women in the Victorian era

## Activity 1: Provoke the Discussion Through Ranking

Show students the poem 'I'm Nobody! Who Are You?' by Emily Dickinson. It would be useful for this poem to be displayed for the whole class to discuss and explore. An audio recording should be used and/or a film clip from *A Quiet Passion*.

> *I'm nobody! Who are you?*
> *Are you nobody, too?*
> *Then there's a pair of us – don't tell!*
> *They'd banish us, you know.*
>
> *How dreary to be somebody!*
> *How public, like a frog*
> *To tell your name the livelong day*
> *To an admiring bog!*

1891, *Poems, Series 2.*

**Download the activity cards at http://resources.corwin.com/learningchallengelessons**

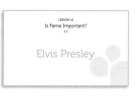

LESSON 14
Is Fame Important?
1-1

Elvis Presley

LESSON 14
Is Fame Important?
1-2

Harry Potter

Choose 12 of the **Activity 1 resource cards**. It is important that there should be some people here with whom the students are not familiar. In pairs/groups, ask students to rank the people named on the cards. You may wish to add or subtract from the list according to your context. You could include your own name to provoke extra discussion!

This activity should help students clarify and define the terms above, bringing in ideas of the public vs. private and the main concept of fame.

- Ask your students to rank the cards from 'somebody' to 'nobody'.
- Ask your students to work in small groups to research the people named on the cards.
- Finally, ask your students to re-rank the cards based on the same ranking criteria.

### Questions for Students

- What makes someone a somebody?
- What makes someone a nobody?
- Who decides if someone is a somebody/nobody?
- Can a person be a somebody and a nobody?
- Isn't everybody a somebody?
- If everyone is a somebody, do nobodies exist?
- If I don't know who they are, can they still be a somebody?
- Can a fictional character be a somebody?
- Did any of your nobodies become somebodies after the research?

## 2. CHALLENGE STUDENTS' UNDERSTANDING OF THE CONCEPT

Here are some examples of cognitive conflict we expect your students to experience:

| Opinion | Conflicting Opinion |
| --- | --- |
| People become famous by possessing extraordinary talents. | There are many talented people who are not famous. |
| Fame must be achieved through hard work and effort. | Some people can be born famous, such as royal family members, children of celebrities or heirs to successful businesses. |
| To be famous means you are well known to the masses. | Some successful business people or social media users are famous only in very specific circles. Many successful song writers and authors would not be recognised even on TV. |
| Famous people are rich. | The famous American writer Edgar Allen Poe was poor for most of his life and struggled to support his family. Outside of the top leagues, sports players are not well paid but are still famous. |
| Fame is fragile and short lived. | Many people are still famous long after they have died, e.g. painters such as Van Gogh and writers such as Charles Dickens. |
| Fame and celebrity are the same thing. | You can have famous buildings, books or pieces of art, but they are not celebrities. |

### Questions for Challenge

- What is fame?
- What makes someone famous?
- Who decides if someone is famous?
- Do famous people always have a famous face?
- How do we know if someone is famous?
- How do we measure fame?

- How do you become famous?
- Can anyone become famous?
- What does fame do for us?
- Is fame something we can always control?
- Is fame always fair?
- Does fame always change people?
- To what extent do you change when you become famous?
- Should fame change people?
- Is fame always a choice?
- When is fame a negative state?
- How important is fame in today's society?
- Are important people always famous?
- Does fame make people important?
- Is it possible to be famous and unimportant?
- Can you be a nobody and be famous?
- Can you be famous and anonymous?
- What can we learn from fame?
- Why do some people want to be famous?
- Should everyone want to be famous?
- Without fame, would we never learn about brilliant people?
- Is fame the reward for hard work?
- How else can we get recognition and reward other than by being famous?
- Does fame always make you rich?
- Do famous people deserve privacy?
- What is the difference between fame and infamy?
- What if you achieve fame after your death?
- What if fame didn't exist?
- What if everyone in the world was famous?

## Questions to Promote Further Dialogue

- Was Emily Dickinson famous?
- Is Emily Dickinson famous now?
- How can we measure her fame then and now?
- Would we have learnt about Emily Dickinson without fame?
- Was fame important to Emily Dickinson?
- Did she want to be famous?
- How was fame different in her lifetime?
- Was fame important in her lifetime?
- Was Dickinson writing the poems for herself or for others to read? Did she want her ideas to be heard?

- Why did some of Dickinson's friends want her to publish? What would this have achieved?

- Would fame have changed her?

- Has fame changed her?

- Did women have the same freedoms as men to publish and present their ideas to the world?

- Was Dickinson scared of becoming a celebrity?

- Why did Dickinson keep a record and make copies of her poems?

- Did Dickinson want to be famous for not publishing her poems?

- Dickinson mocks the idea of fame and the public domain, but there are claims that she still sent some of her poems to important publishers. How does this affect our view of her?

- Why did she *continue* to correspond with publishers and writers if she didn't want fame?

- Did she want friendship rather than fame?

- If Emily Dickinson and her work had not become famous, would this have been a tragedy?

- Some editors were unhappy with Dickinson's use of punctuation and altered her poems for publication. Could this explain her reluctance to publish?

- Could Dickinson have remained authentic if she had become famous?

- Is authenticity more important than fame?

- Why did Dickinson publish her poems anonymously? Does this suggest a rejection of fame or a fear of rejection?

- Why didn't Emily Dickinson publish more of her poems anonymously?

- Would Dickinson have published more poems if Thomas Higginson had encouraged her to do so at the start of their correspondence?

- Has fame allowed us to see and share Dickinson's brilliance or has fame intruded on and exposed a private individual?

- Does fame provide recognition and reward?

- Did Emily Dickinson want recognition and reward?

# 3. CONSTRUCT UNDERSTANDING

### Activity 2: Venn Diagram

Distribute **Activity 2 Orange resource cards,** which contain details on the life of Emily Dickinson. Ask students to sort through the cards and answer the following question:

**Was fame important to Emily Dickinson?**

It is useful to support your students when they are sorting through the information in front of them. This can help them to interpret and handle the information more easily, and reconstruct their thinking in order to reach an understanding.

The resources can be sorted into piles or into two large hoops on the floor, labelled as shown on the Venn Diagram at the top of the opposite page. They should be encouraged to talk about the criteria they are using to sort the resources.

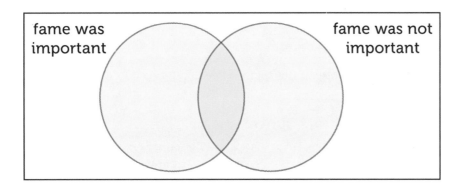

LESSON 14
Is Fame Important?
2-7

She sent some of her poems to editors and publishers such as Samuel Bowles (owner and editor of the *Springfield Republican* newspaper) and Thomas Wentworth Higginson (frequent contributor to the *Atlantic Monthly* magazine).

Now you can distribute the **Activity 2 Blue resource cards**, which contain details and information from the letters that Emily Dickinson sent to various correspondents. Ask students to continue to sort and classify these. Again, students should be encouraged to talk about the criteria they are using to sort the resources.

The third set of resources contain the names of four poems by Emily Dickinson that explore ideas on fame. Distribute these **Activity 2 Green resource cards** to different pairings/small groups and ask your students to explore each poem and look for clues which confirm or contradict their opinion so far.

LESSON 14
Is Fame Important?
2-30

'Publication is foreign to my thought.'

Letter from Emily Dickinson to Thomas Higginson.

Depending on the size of your room, you could divide the area into four zones so your students can move around the room, studying each poem in turn and sharing ideas. Alternatively, you could just give one poem per group leading to a shared discussion where students feed back on their findings.

After this activity, bring the class together and ask each pair/group to present their findings to help answer the question: Was fame important to Emily Dickinson?

LESSON 14
Is Fame Important?
2-42

"Fame is the one that does not stay–" (1507)

### Activity 3: Opinion Line

Your students could present their ideas and explore their thinking using an Opinion Line with respect to the statement 'Fame was important to Emily Dickinson'.

Evidence can be used from the first and second activities to support and justify reasoning and opinions.

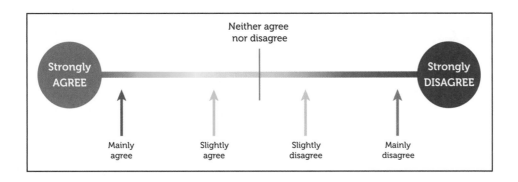

### Adaptation

You could reduce the number of cards or resources your students are categorising at any one time. They can also be provided with a number of possible definitions that they can consider and evaluate.

### Extension

Ask your students to create a Concept Corner Chart to build on their understanding of fame.

| | |
|---|---|
| Examples of phrases or sentences where fame is used:<br>Wall of fame<br>Rise to fame | Examples of contexts where fame applies:<br>Celebrity<br>Media<br>Film industry |
| Examples of words or phrases of similar or opposite meaning to fame:<br>Infamy<br>Stardom<br>Disgrace<br>Obscurity | Examples of related ideas or associations:<br>Film<br>Art<br>Sport |

*Fame*

Ask students to create a timeline of Emily Dickinson's life to help us understand her history, experiences and environment when writing poetry. This timeline could be used to examine whether Dickinson's views about fame changed across time.

Allocate one of Emily Dickinson's poems on fame to pairs or small groups and ask them to create a podcast for other students to explain how fame is represented.

## 4. CONSIDER THE LEARNING JOURNEY

At the end of the activity it is usual to encourage the students to review their learning journey and the thinking process they have engaged in throughout the session.

This can include reflection on the thinking that has taken place to this point, and a summary and conclusion of the new understanding reached.

Explicit reference to Learning Intentions and Success Criteria is a good starting point for this reflection, but it is also helpful to return to and re-examine some key questions.

- How has our understanding of the concept of 'fame' changed over the course of this lesson?

- Should fame be important?

- Was fame important to Emily Dickinson?

- Does your understanding of the concept and importance of fame differ from that of Emily Dickinson?

- Has this lesson deepened your understanding of these specific examples of Emily Dickinson's view on fame?

## Ideas for Transfer

Encourage students to investigate other poets whose work touches upon the concept of 'fame' such as John Keats's 'On Fame' and John Clare's 'Idle Fame'. This could lead to a Jigsaw activity where groups are allocated a key poem that they have to research and then teach to the rest of the class.

Broaden students' understanding of Emily Dickinson's poetry by exploring the different themes of her poetry, such as death, nature, friendship and love.

Ask your students to create their own Hall of Fame where they identify a small selection of individuals whom they believe should belong there. They could write short biographies on the people they have chosen and explain why their chosen person belongs in the Hall of Fame. They could use **Activity 1 resource cards** for this activity.

Your students could investigate how individuals have risen and then fallen from fame and the reasons for this. Students could explore this theme by using popular websites.

# WWW•EBI

## WWW – What Worked Well . . .

## EBI – Even Better If . . .

# LESSON
# 15

# Was Wilfred Owen a Patriot or a Pacifist?

**KEY CONCEPTS:** Patriotism, Pacifism

**KEY SKILLS:** Analysing the use of language in poetry

Determining themes in poetry

Analysing the representation of a theme across multiple texts

Citing textual evidence

# Was Wilfred Owen a Patriot or a Pacifist?

## OVERVIEW:

This lesson will enhance students' knowledge and understanding of the terms 'patriotism' and 'pacifism' to gain insight into the views of Wilfred Owen and other war poets. It would be useful for the students to be familiar with the war poet Wilfred Owen and to have some understanding of poetic terminology.

## KEY CONCEPTS:

Patriotism

Pacifism

## KEY WORDS:

War, conflict, loyalty, honour, peace, dedication, politics, individual vs. society, responsibility, love, suffering, allegiance, support and betrayal.

## LEARNING INTENTION:

To be able to define patriotism and pacifism and identify examples of this in poetry.

## SUCCESS CRITERIA:

We can do the following:

- Explore and discuss our understanding of the terms 'patriotism' and 'pacifism'.

- Classify symbols, images and quotes that are connected to the key concepts.

- Look for clues within extracts of war poetry that show us ideas and attitudes related to patriotism and pacifism.

- Identify evidence in Wilfred Owen's poetry and letters that helps us understand his views on war.

- Decide if Wilfred Owen was a patriot or a pacifist.

## STRATEGIES USED:

Venn Diagram

Mystery

Jigsaw Groups

# 1. IDENTIFY IMPORTANT CONCEPTS

Some of the key areas to investigate within and around the concepts of 'patriotism' and 'pacifism' are the following:

- War
- Justice
- Morality
- Individual vs. society
- Protection
- Safety
- Peace
- Loyalty
- Responsibility
- Nobility
- Suffering
- Death
- Sacrifice
- Duty

# 2. CHALLENGE STUDENTS' UNDERSTANDING OF THE CONCEPT

Here are some examples of cognitive conflict we expect your students to experience.

| Opinion | Conflicting Opinion |
|---|---|
| Patriots and pacifists are complete opposites. | It is possible to be patriotic and a pacifist at the same time.<br>For example, 'I don't want to sacrifice our young soldiers in a foreign war.' |
| Pacifists object to conflict in all situations. | You can be a pacifist only in relation to certain conflicts.<br>For example, 'We should fight invaders but not be invaders.' |
| Patriotism means always putting your country first. | You can be patriotic because of the freedom your country gives you to put *yourself* first. |
| Pacifists aren't brave. | Some pacifists have been willing to die for what they believe. |
| Patriotism means thinking that your country is the best. | Patriots can admire all nations and peoples of the world. |
| Patriotism demonstrates loyalty. | I am loyal to my friend, but that doesn't mean I'm a patriot. |

### Questions for Challenge

- What is patriotism?
- What is pacifism?
- What are the differences between patriotism and pacifism?
- What makes someone a patriot or a pacifist?
- What makes someone a patriot *and* a pacifist?
- Can you be neither a patriot nor a pacifist?
- What makes someone a pacifist but not a patriot?
- Could you be a patriot if you disagreed with war?
- Does everyone have a duty to be patriotic?
- Which is more important – a duty to one's country or a duty to ourselves?
- Should we always be loyal to our country?
- Should we always agree with the views and actions of our government?
- What if we were all patriots or all pacifists?
- Are the decisions governments make always for the benefit of their county and its citizens?
- Does fighting for your country make you a patriot?
- Is it possible for a soldier to be a pacifist?
- Is it possible to be a patriot and a pacifist at the same time?
- When is patriotism a bad thing and when is it a good thing?
- When is pacifism a bad thing and when is it a good thing?
- What evidence is there that pacifists love their country?
- What if there was no patriotism?
- What if there was no pacifism?
- What is the difference between patriotism and nationalism?
- When does patriotism aid peace?
- When does pacifism create conflict?
- What is the difference between a pacifist and a conscientious objector?
- When should pacifists not be conscientious objectors?

## 3. CONSTRUCT UNDERSTANDING

### Activity 1: Venn Diagram

Distribute the **Activity 1 Orange resource cards** to pairs or small groups. Ask your students to sort and classify the cards into things linked to patriotism and things linked to pacifism.

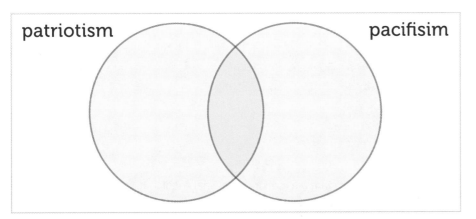

patriotism

pacifisim

**Download the activity cards at http://resources.corwin.com/learningchallengelessons**

Image source: LittlePerfectStock/ Shutterstock.com

If your students begin to populate the cross-over section of the Venn Diagram, ask them:

How is possible for something to be linked to patriotism and pacifism?

Your students can be encouraged to add their own ideas or images to blank cards. Once the cards have been sorted, students can work together to complete the sentences below to demonstrate their understanding of pacifism and patriotism.

Patriotism is . . .

Pacifism is . . .

Once the teacher feels that the students have a clear grasp of the terms 'patriotism' and 'pacifism', the **Activity 1 Blue resource cards** can be distributed where students read and study lines of poetry from a range of poets.

Encourage your students to explore what the language and devices reveal about the poets' views and add these extracts to the sorted patriotism and pacifism sets.

## Activity 2: Mystery

A Mystery is a useful tool for challenging the thinking of students. Distribute the **Activity 2 resource cards** to groups of 3–4, and encourage your students to use the evidence on those cards to answer the following question:

**Was Wilfred Owen a patriot or a pacifist?**

It is often useful to support the students when they are sorting through the information in front of them. This can help them to interpret and handle the information more easily, and reconstruct their thinking to reach an understanding.

| Evidence to show that Wilfred Owen was a patriot. | Evidence to show that Wilfred Owen was a pacifist. | Evidence that is not relevant. |
|---|---|---|
| | | |

Our conclusion is . . .

The key reasons for this are . . .

### Questions to Promote Further Dialogue

- Could Wilfred Owen have avoided enlisting for war?

- Wilfred Owen fought and died for his country. Does this make him a patriot?

- Was Wilfred Owen loyal to his country?

- Is there a difference between loyalty and patriotism?

- Why did Owen write about war in his poetry?

- Who did Owen write the poems for?

- How did Owen want the reader to feel after reading his poems?

- Does Owen offer an alternative to war?

- Are Owen's actions more important than his words?

- Why did Owen return to the war after getting injured?

- Does Owen's praise of his fellow soldiers suggest patriotism? '. . . you could not be visited by a band of friends half so fine as surround us here.'

- Does Owen present soldiers as brave and noble?

- How does Owen present the government compared to the soldiers?

- Why does Owen address the reader as 'my friend' in *Dulce et Decorum est*?

- What did Owen want to 'warn' his readers about? Did he have a moral purpose?

- Does Owen's opinion of war change?

- Is Wilfred Owen a war hero? Does this affect our view of whether he was a patriot or a pacifist?

- 'Above all I am concerned with poetry. My subject is War, and the pity of War. The poetry is in the pity.' How far do you agree that Owen was true to this statement?

### Adaptation

You or your students could select a smaller range of cards for the Venn Diagram activity.

### Extension

To add extra challenge to **Activity 1**, give some students blank cards so they can add extra ideas and symbols to represent patriotism and pacifism.

Students could create a timeline using the cards from the Mystery activity, matching historical information and poetry extracts. Students could be encouraged to explore **how** and **if** Owen's attitudes to war changed over time.

Timelines could be created on:

- Wilfred Owen's life, 1893–1918.

- 1914–1918 when Owen wrote most of his most famous war poems.

To promote discussion on Owen's different views of war, the students could be encouraged to compare the poem *'Apologia Pro Poemate Meo'* with poems such as 'Disabled', 'Anthem for Doomed Youth' or *'Dulce et Decorum est'*. They could lift quotes from these poems that show examples of either patriotic or pacifistic writing.

Having explored this concept, you could ask your students to plan and write an essay in response to the key question.

# 4. CONSIDER THE LEARNING JOURNEY

At the end of the activity it is usual to encourage the students to review their learning journey and the thinking process they have engaged in throughout the session.

This can include reflection on the thinking that has taken place to this point and a summary and conclusion of the new understanding reached.

They can do this by returning to and re-examining some key questions:

- What have we learnt about the terms 'patriotism' and 'pacifism'?

- Do you believe you can be both a patriot and a pacifist?

- Was Wilfred Owen a patriot or a pacifist?

- What questions do you still have?

## Ideas for Transfer: Jigsaw Groups

In pairs or groups, students could explore and analyse the political speeches of Barack Obama. His speech, 'The America We Love' (June 2008), addresses the term 'patriotism'.

- Split the speech into equal sections and allocate each section to a pair/group.

- Encourage each pair/group to explore how the speaker presents the term 'patriotism'.

- Challenge each group to explore how the speaker uses language to present his ideas.

- Each group shares their findings and teaches the rest of the class.

Your students could write their own poem that reflects their own views on patriotism and pacifism. They could use the same techniques employed by war poets they have studied in this activity.

Encourage your students to explore and study how the media play a role in promoting pacifism and patriotism.

# WWW•EBI

## WWW – What Worked Well . . .

## EBI – Even Better If . . .

The Lesson Ideas

LESSON

# 16

# Does the Poem 'The Road Not Taken' Show Us How to Make the Right Choice?

**KEY CONCEPT:** Choice

**KEY SKILLS:** Analysing the use of language in poetry

Determining theme in poetry

Analysing author's word choice in conveying a theme or idea

Citing textual evidence

# Does the Poem 'The Road Not Taken' Show Us How to Make the Right Choice?

## OVERVIEW:

This lesson on 'The Road Not Taken' by Robert Frost will enhance students' knowledge and understanding of how Robert Frost presents the concept of 'choice'. It would be beneficial to allow your students to read this poem ahead of the lesson as a preview to the activities that follow.

## KEY CONCEPT:

Choice

## KEY WORDS:

Choice, decision, dilemma, consequence, influence, outcome, journey, travel, selection, preference and predicament.

## LEARNING INTENTION:

To understand how Robert Frost presents the concept of choice in 'The Road Not Taken'.

## SUCCESS CRITERIA:

We can do the following:

- Explore and examine the concept of 'choice' and the 'right' choice.

- Consider the concept of 'choice' as a key theme within a work of poetry.

- Identify how the poem presents the concept of 'choice'.

- Analyse and discuss the language at different stages in the poem to determine what we learn about choice.

- Decide if the poem shows us how to make the 'right' choice.

## STRATEGIES USED:

Opinion Corners

Mystery

Opinion Line

# 1. IDENTIFY IMPORTANT CONCEPTS

Some of the key areas to investigate within and around the concept of 'choice' are the following:

- Choice and options

- Choice and free will

- Choice and influence

- Extrinsic and intrinsic influences on our choices

- Decision making

- Good choices vs. bad choices

- Choice and outcomes

- Choice and consequences

- Reversible and irreversible choices

- The absence of choice

# 2. CHALLENGE STUDENTS' UNDERSTANDING OF THE CONCEPT

Here are some examples of the cognitive conflict we expect your students to experience:

| Opinion | Conflicting Opinion |
| --- | --- |
| I always have a choice. | Some things I have to do because I am told to. |
| It is harder to make a choice when you only have two things to choose between. | It is harder to choose when you have lots of things to choose between. |
| A choice you feel good about is the right choice. | You can feel good about a choice, but it can still be the wrong choice. |
| I'm free to choose. | My choices are influenced. |
| We make the right choices if we think about them properly. | We can think about a choice long and hard and still make the wrong choice. |

## Questions for Challenge

- What is choice?

- How do we know what a choice is?

- How do we know what the right choice is?

- What's the difference between a choice and the right choice?

- How do we make choices and right choices?

- What can we choose?

- What can't we choose?

- Should we always make the right choice?

- Who provides the choices?

- Is there always just one right choice?
- How and when do we know that we've made a bad choice?
- What if we weren't given a choice and somebody else decided for us?
- Should we ever let anyone make our choices for us?
- What should we base our choices on?
- How do we know if a particular choice is more important than others?
- Who or what has the most influence on our choices?
- Who or what *should* influence our choices?
- What do we have to know before making the right choice?
- Is it always possible to make the right choice?
- Is the right choice always the best choice?
- Can we make the right choice if we don't know the consequences?
- When is choice a bad thing?
- Who decides if a choice is good or bad?
- Can we always know if the choice is right or wrong?
- Can a wrong choice turn out positively? Does this make it the right choice?
- What is the difference between a choice and a decision?
- Who do we make choices for?
- When don't we have a right to choose?
- Do we create our own choices?
- Are our choices pre-determined?
- What is the relationship between choice and risk?
- To what extent do choices change our lives?
- How might we be fooled into making a certain choice?
- Is a choice ever a sacrifice? What might we sacrifice when we make a choice?
- How would the right choice be a sacrifice if the choice improves our life?
- How is a choice an opportunity?
- Is every choice a sacrifice or an opportunity?
- Can you think deeply about a choice or decision but still make a mistake?
- If a choice becomes a mistake, is that because we haven't thought about it well enough?
- Do choices always have consequences?
- Can you make a choice without there being any consequences?
- Should choices always be thought about?
- Do we always need to be mindful of the consequences of our choices?
- Should we follow our heart or our head? Is it okay to make a choice based on the toss of a coin?
- Should we always be confident about our choices?
- Should choices always be made decisively?

- Does age and experience equip people to make wiser choices?

- If you reflect positively on a choice, does that always mean it was the best choice?

- In life, is the 'path of least resistance' always the best choice?

- Will you make, or have you made, the right choices during this lesson?

- Do all journeys involve choices?

## Questions for Further Dialogue

- How does the speaker in the poem feel about choices?

- Frost originally titled his poem 'Two Roads'. Why do you think he chose a different title and how does this affect our view of choices in the poem?

- Why does the writer use a metaphor of a road rather than a path?

- What factors influence the speaker in their choices?

- How does the (description of) appearance of the two roads affect the speaker's choice?

- Why can't the speaker travel down both roads?

- Why is the speaker sad that he can't travel down both roads?

- Why does the speaker try to look ahead in lines 4 and 5 of the first stanza?

- How does the narrator make his choice on which road to follow?

- Does the speaker have any other choices in the poem?

- What if the speaker hadn't chosen either road?

- How are the speaker's choices limited?

- Is the speaker choosing his own road or a road decided by others before him?

- Why does the speaker doubt that he'll return to the other road?

- What does doubt reveal about making the right choices in life?

- How confident does the speaker feel about his choice?

- What struggles does the speaker face when making the choice?

- What does the speaker's indecision show us about making right choices?

- How is the speaker's indecision important in understanding the concept of 'choices' and 'right' choices?

- Does the speaker feel he has made the right choice?

- What does the speaker learn about choices and right choices in the poem?

- What *don't* we learn about choice?

- Does the writer in 'The Road Not Taken' convey any sense that his character feels (or felt) an obligation towards a certain choice?

- How does the speaker feel about the road he chose? What is the tone of the speaker in the third stanza? And in the fourth stanza, what does the speaker mean by 'sigh'?

- Does the speaker understand the consequences of his choice?

- Is this lesson about poetry or a journey or about something else?

- How has the speaker changed because of this choice? How will the speaker reflect on his choice in the future?

- Is it possible for the speaker to make the right choice?

- Should we view the poem as about choice or indecision?

- Why do you think some people mistakenly call the poem 'The Road Less Travelled'?

- What do you think Robert Frost wanted us to understand about choice?

- How can we evaluate the choices made in 'A Road Not Taken'?

# 3. CONSTRUCT UNDERSTANDING

**Download the activity cards at http://resources.corwin.com/learningchallengelessons**

### Activity 1: Opinion Corner

Opinion Corners require students to make an exact choice. They are very useful for developing not only skills of reasoning and explanation, but also the language of persuasion.

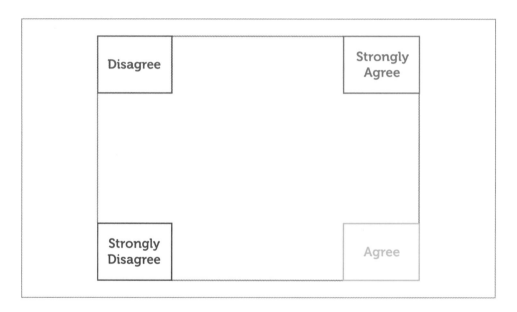

After you read a statement from the **Activity 1 resource cards**, your students should stand in the corner that best represents their opinion.

Use one or more of the statements available, but not all of them.

Once your students have chosen a corner, get them to talk about their choice with the people around them. A spokesperson from each corner should give a summary representing the views of the people standing in that corner.

### Activity 2: Mystery

Divide your class into groups of 3–4 and present them with the following key question:

**Does the poem 'The Road Not Taken' show us how to make the right choice?**

Distribute **Activity 2 resource cards** containing lines from the poem, historical detail and ideas on the concept of choice. Your students should read through the cards and discuss how the evidence can help us to answer the question above.

It is useful to support your students when they are sorting through the information in front of them. This can help them to interpret and handle the information more easily and reconstruct their thinking in order to reach an understanding.

| Evidence to demonstrate that the poem does show us how to make the right choice. | Evidence to demonstrate that the poem doesn't show us how to make the right choice. | Evidence that is not relevant. |
| --- | --- | --- |
| | | |
| Our conclusion is . . . | | |
| The key reasons for this are . . . | | |

### Questions for Further Dialogue

- How does the speaker make their choice?
- Does the speaker feel they have made the right choice in the poem?
- What do we learn about 'right choices' from the poem?
- Can we see the right choice in the poem?
- Can we judge the right choice in the poem?

### Activity 3: Opinion Line

Your students could present their ideas and explore their thinking using an Opinion Line. Evidence can be used from the first and second activities to support and justify reasoning and opinions.

Ask your students to respond to the following statement:

**The poem 'The Road Not Taken' shows us how to make the right choice.**

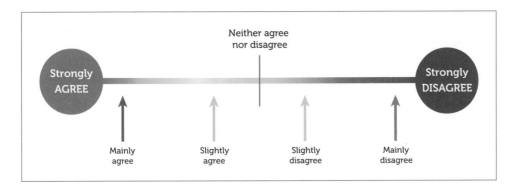

### Adaptation

You could reduce the number of cards or resources your students are categorising at any one time. They can also be provided with a number of possible definitions that they can consider and evaluate.

### Extension

Ask your students to identify and rank the most important factors that influence our choices. This list could be generated by your students or the teacher could provide a selection to choose from, such as love, money, family, friends, fear, peer pressure, social media, appearance, political views, time, the past and the future.

Having explored this concept, you could ask your students to plan and write an essay in response to the key question.

## 4. CONSIDER THE LEARNING JOURNEY

At the end of the activity it is worthwhile to encourage the students to review their learning journey and the thinking process they have participated in throughout the lesson.

This can consist of reflection on the thinking that has taken place by summarising and concluding on their new-found understanding.

Explicit reference to Learning Intentions and Success Criteria is a good starting point for this reflection, but it is also helpful to consider some of the following questions:

- What is your understanding of the concept of 'choice' and 'right choices'?
- How did Robert Frost's poetry help you to understand the concept of 'choice' and how to make the 'right' choice?
- Have the activities you've undertaken over the course of this lesson deepened your understanding of the concept and the poem?
- Has anyone changed their mind about what choice is and what right choices are?
- What do you know now that you didn't know before?
- What questions do you still have?
- Which idea really made you think?
- Did you choose the right road in this lesson?

### Ideas for Transfer

To gain a deeper understanding of Robert Frost and his poems, your students could explore his life history and literary influences. It would be beneficial for your students to examine more of his poems, such as 'Stopping by Woods on a Snowy Evening'. Using a Venn Diagram, your students could compare these two poems, exploring themes, language, devices, form and structure.

Encourage your students to explore the choices made by characters in literature or historical figures. Your students could create a Venn Diagram with one circle labelled **right choices** and the second labelled **wrong choices**.

Ask your students to discuss and reflect on the important choices (good or bad!) they have made in the past. If they feel comfortable doing so, they could share the consequences of these actions. They could also share important choices they will need to make in the future.

Your students could create a diagram demonstrating the choices they will face in the future with two roads (or more!). On these roads, your students could write their feelings about each choice and decide on how the roads would appear.

Ask your students to create a diary entry on the right or wrong choices they have made in the past and the consequences of this choice.

Invite your students to create a short video that informs younger students about the important choices they will need to make in their lives.

## The Road Not Taken

*Two roads diverged in a yellow wood,*

*And sorry I could not travel both*

*And be one traveler, long I stood*

*And looked down one as far as I could*

*To where it bent in the undergrowth;*

*Then took the other, as just as fair,*

*And having perhaps the better claim,*

*Because it was grassy and wanted wear;*

*Though as for that the passing there*

*Had worn them really about the same,*

*And both that morning equally lay*

*In leaves no step had trodden black.*

*Oh, I kept the first for another day!*

*Yet knowing how way leads on to way,*

*I doubted if I should ever come back.*

*I shall be telling this with a sigh*

*Somewhere ages and ages hence:*

*Two roads diverged in a wood, and I –*

*I took the one less traveled by,*

*And that has made all the difference*

(Robert Frost, 1874–1963)

# WWW•EBI

## WWW – What Worked Well . . .

## EBI – Even Better If . . .

# LESSON 17

# Was the Californian Gold Rush of 1848 the Main Cause of Conflict Between Native and European Americans?

**KEY CONCEPT:** Conflict

**KEY SKILLS:** Analysing the main ideas of a primary or secondary source

Identifying the author's point of view in an informational text

Demonstrating an understanding of vocabulary specific to history/social studies

# Was the Californian Gold Rush of 1848 the Main Cause of Conflict Between Native and European Americans?

## OVERVIEW:

It is essential that students have read extracts from Dee Brown's *Bury My Heart at Wounded Knee: An Indian History of the American West*. It would be beneficial for students to have an emerging understanding of Native American history.

## KEY CONCEPT:

Conflict

## KEY WORDS:

Conflict, war, expansionism, racism, genocide, Manifest Destiny, freedom, equality, oppression, pioneers, colonisation, ethnic cleansing, native, resources, conquest, human rights, xenophobia and propaganda.

## LEARNING INTENTION:

To understand the significant factors contributing to the 19th-century conflict between Native and European Americans.

## SUCCESS CRITERIA:

We can do the following:

- Define conflict in its various forms.

- Examine extracts from Dee Brown's text and infer from the language used some possible causes of the conflict.

- Question and assess the significance of the gold rush as a cause of the conflict.

- Explore other possible causes of the conflict.

- Evaluate and justify the impact that each cause had upon the people and the landscape of the American West.

- Identify how the causes of the conflict are interconnected and formulate a hypothesis to support our thinking.

## STRATEGIES USED:

Mystery

Opinion Line

# 1. IDENTIFY IMPORTANT CONCEPTS

Some of the key areas to investigate within and around the concept of 'conflict' are the following:

- Religious beliefs
- Human rights
- Political and social freedom
- Oppression
- Racism
- Equality
- Rivalry
- Competition
- War
- Fighting
- Threats
- Xenophobia
- Conquest
- Colonisation
- Expansionism
- Internal and external conflict
- Inner and outer conflict

# 2. CHALLENGE STUDENTS' UNDERSTANDING OF THE CONCEPT

Here are some examples of cognitive conflict we expect your students to experience:

| Opinion | Conflicting Opinion |
|---|---|
| Those who treat others badly deserve to be treated badly in return. | 'An eye for an eye only ends up making the whole world blind.' Mahatma Gandhi. |
| If I don't stand up for myself, I will be considered weak. | It takes a lot of strength to turn your back and walk away from conflict. |
| Conflict restores order and allows free nations to exist. | If a tyrannical nation is victorious, then they can do whatever they want to the nation they have conquered. |
| Conflict is destructive and nothing positive ever comes from it. | Conflict can be constructive by driving competition and accelerating progress in technology (e.g. aviation) that will still be beneficial long after the conflict is over. |
| Conflict is an unavoidable part of life. | There is always a peaceful resolution to something if you look for it. |

## Questions for Challenge

- What is conflict?
- How do we define conflict?
- What causes conflict?
- How might we see, hear or feel conflict?
- Does conflict always result in violence?
- Ronald Reagan said, 'Peace is not absence of conflict; it is the ability to handle conflict by peaceful means.' How true is this statement?
- Is it possible to achieve peace through compromise?
- When might compromise be a sign of weakness?
- When could conflict be justified?
- Is violence never justified?
- How can conflict be resolved?
- When might conflict be a good thing?
- What if conflict cannot be resolved?
- Is it possible to experience conflict within ourselves?
- Should we ever become involved in the conflicts of others?
- Is it always important to remember past conflicts?
- How do we learn from the mistakes of the past?
- Does history always repeat itself?
- What is at the heart of most conflicts?
- If you believe you are right, does that mean others are wrong?
- Are there always two sides to every conflict?
- How might conflict be damaging?
- How can conflict be avoided?
- What if conflict didn't exist?
- How does conflict affect your life?

## Questions for Further Dialogue

- Why was the story of the Native Americans rarely heard?
- Should Dee Brown's text be read by every American?
- What was Dee Brown's purpose in producing *Bury My Heart at Wounded Knee*?
- How powerful is the language used by Dee Brown?
- How does Dee Brown's use of pathos help engage the reader?
- How useful is oral history?
- Why do you think Dee Brown's *Bury My Heart at Wounded Knee* became a best seller?

# 3. CONSTRUCT UNDERSTANDING

### Activity 1: Mystery

Introduce the following question:

**Was the Californian Gold Rush of 1848 the main cause of conflict between Native and European Americans?**

Divide your students into small groups and distribute **Activity 1 resource cards** to each group.

Ask your students to sort the cards using their own criteria. Often it is helpful to offer support and structure to students when they are sorting and classifying information. This can help with their understanding of the content and support a higher level of analysis and interpretation.

## Possible Criteria

- Primary sources
- Irrelevant cards
- Gold Rush
- Manifest Destiny
- Railroad expansion
- Unemployment
- Propaganda

Your students should be encouraged to be reflective throughout the exercise. They can change the criteria they choose to sort by if they don't feel they are effective in helping them answer the question, and they should actively be exploring possible routes to constructing a reasoned answer.

Encourage each group to share their analysis and to offer critical but constructive feedback.

A Consider Chart can help them to assimilate their thinking:

online resources

**Download the activity cards at http://resources.corwin.com/learningchallengelessons**

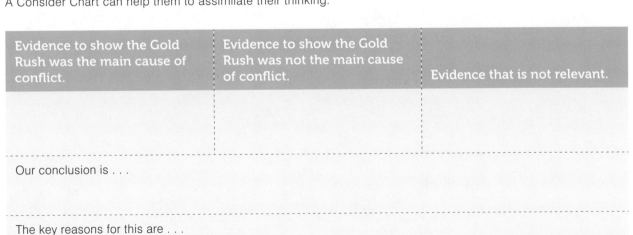

| Evidence to show the Gold Rush was the main cause of conflict. | Evidence to show the Gold Rush was not the main cause of conflict. | Evidence that is not relevant. |
| --- | --- | --- |
| | | |

Our conclusion is . . .

The key reasons for this are . . .

## Activity 2: Opinion Line

Having considered the causes of conflict and the struggle for the plains in the 19th century, your students are now challenged to consider literary intent, historical opinion and bias. By using an Opinion Line, they can now analyse historical perceptions and beliefs.

Ask your students to work in pairs or small groups. Give each group a character and ask them to take on the persona of that character. They are to consider the beliefs and values that each character may have. Each pair or group are to stand on the Opinion Line and explain to what extent they agree or disagree with the following statement:

The Californian Gold Rush of 1848 was the main cause of conflict between Native and European Americans.

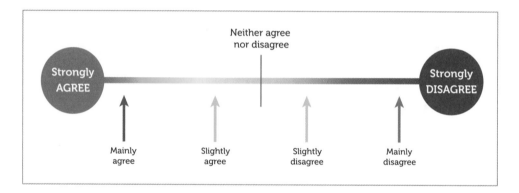

After each group have presented their argument and placed themselves upon the continuum, the remaining students can offer feedback and challenge each other's opinions.

Encourage your students to refer to historical sources such as *Bury My Heart at Wounded Knee*.

Possible character roles:

- President Jackson
- Sitting Bull
- Crazy Horse
- A cattle rancher
- A homesteader
- A 49er
- Dee Brown
- A US military officer
- A medicine man/Indian Shaman

### Adaptation

Fewer cards could be used.

Use more picture images to depict the causes of conflict.

Visual or audio sources could be used to depict the conflict. Excellent examples are the 2007 adaption of *Bury My Heart at Wounded Knee* and Kevin Costner's *Dances with Wolves*.

## Extension

Include some blank cards for students to add their own commentary or quotes.

Ask your students to find further evidence in Dee Brown's text to answer the question.

Introduce further written accounts of the conflict such as John Ehle's *Trail of Tears* and ask students to add extracts to the Mystery.

Students could write up their findings of the Mystery in essay form.

# 4. CONSIDER THE LEARNING JOURNEY

At the end of the activity it is usual to encourage your students to review their learning journey and the thinking process they have engaged in throughout the session.

This can include reflection on the thinking that has taken place to this point and a summary and conclusion of the new understanding reached.

Explicit reference to Learning Intentions and Success Criteria is a good starting point for this reflection, but it is also helpful to return to and re-examine some key questions:

- What do you understand about the concept of 'conflict'?
- Do you think Dee Brown's purpose in producing a text on Native American history was to explore conflict?
- How do you view the policy of American expansionism in the 19th century and the conflict that was caused?
- What can we learn from the conflict between the Native and European Americans?
- What questions do you have following today's lesson?
- What will you remember about today's lesson?
- What skills have you used during today's lesson? When and where would you use them again?

## Ideas for Transfer

Ask your students to generate examples of daily conflicts that they may face. Using a Venn Diagram, ask your students to organise potential daily conflicts in their personal lives into internal and external conflicts.

In groups, your students could create some conflict cards. Each card will contain an example of a conflict. These cards could be shuffled and then re-distributed throughout the class. The challenge would be for each group to then formulate a solution for each conflict card.

Ask your students to create a guide to the Gold Rush conflict for younger children. This could be in the form of a cartoon or short story.

# WWW•EBI

## WWW – What Worked Well . . .

## EBI – Even Better If . . .

# Did Anne Frank Experience Happiness?

**KEY CONCEPT:** Happiness

**KEY SKILLS:** Analysing the main ideas of a primary or secondary source
Identifying the author's point of view in an informational text
Demonstrate understanding of vocabulary specific to history/social studies
Citing textual evidence

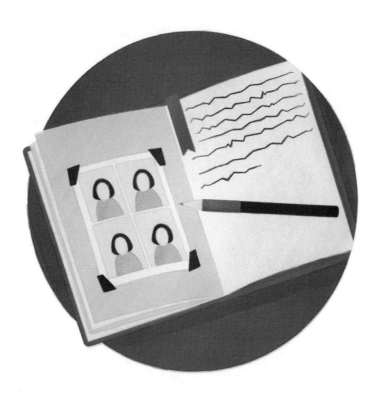

# Did Anne Frank Experience Happiness?

## OVERVIEW:

This lesson will enhance students' knowledge and understanding of Anne Frank and her life during the Second World War and the Nazi occupation. It would be useful for students to be familiar with *The Diary of a Young Girl* prior to starting this activity.

## KEY CONCEPT:

Happiness

## KEY VOCABULARY:

Happiness, loneliness, solitude, isolation, love, relationships, adolescence, genocide, extermination, Holocaust, fear, freedom and injustice.

## LEARNING INTENTION:

To be able to identify and interpret whether Anne Frank experienced happiness during the time documented in her diary.

## SUCCESS CRITERIA:

We can do the following:

- Identify possible definitions of happiness and connect these to the experiences of Anne Frank.

- Analyse the author's use of language to determine her level of happiness.

- Consider and evaluate the impact of happiness/sadness upon the author.

- Reflect on the experiences of happiness in a different time and context in relation to ourselves.

## STRATEGY USED:

Fortune Line

# 1. IDENTIFY IMPORTANT CONCEPTS

Some of the key areas to investigate within and around the concept of 'happiness' are the following:

- The definition of happiness
- The subjective nature of happiness
- Sadness
- Self-awareness
- Happiness over time
- Happiness across cultures
- Age and maturity

# 2. CHALLENGE STUDENTS' UNDERSTANDING OF THE CONCEPT

Here are some examples of cognitive conflict we expect students to experience:

| Opinion | Conflicting Opinion |
|---|---|
| You can tell when someone is happy. | People often pretend to be happy when they are not. |
| Happiness is a choice. | Happiness is a spontaneous response. |
| Happiness comes from within. | External factors influence your happiness. |
| The pursuit of happiness is thought to be a good thing. | Continually pursuing happiness can make you unhappy. |
| You are either a happy person or you are not. | Happiness is a temporary state. |
| Good people are happy people. | Happy people are not always good people. |

## Questions for Challenge

- What is happiness?
- How do you know if you are happy?
- Is it possible to be happy and sad at the same time?
- When is happiness a bad emotion?
- Who decides what happiness is?
- What's the difference between happiness and contentment?
- How could happiness be measured?
- How can people assess their own happiness?
- Can you always tell if a person is happy?
- What is the difference between shared and personal happiness?
- Is happiness always temporary?
- What conditions favour happiness?
- How would you define true happiness?

- Is it possible to experience happiness if you never experience sadness?
- How much influence can you have over your own happiness and sadness?
- Can we influence other people's happiness and sadness?
- What would a recipe for happiness contain?
- What is the cost of happiness?
- Does everyone want to be happy?
- Is the pursuit of happiness a worthwhile endeavour?
- Is it ever pointless to pursue happiness?
- Are we always responsible for our emotions?
- Should happiness be promoted as a good thing?
- What if our happiness makes another person sad?
- What makes us happy?
- Is happiness contagious?
- Which emotion is stronger, happiness or sadness?
- Is there any evidence that we are born happy?
- What could make happiness a habit?
- Are happy people always more successful?

# 3. CONSTRUCT UNDERSTANDING

**Download the activity cards at http://resources.corwin.com/ learningchallengelessons**

### Activity 1: Fortune Line

Students are enquiring into the fortunes of Anne Frank, 1942–1944. Through exploring the concept of 'happiness', students are beginning to examine the impact this emotion has upon the author's life. By plotting key events and textual evidence upon

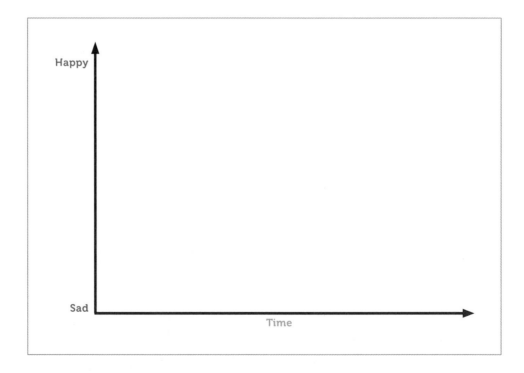

a graph, students are challenged to make logical inferences from the text and to reach substantiated conclusions.

Students are presented with **Activity 1 resource cards**; each card displays an event or quotation relating to Anne Frank's life. Students are also presented with a graph called a Fortune Line. The x-axis of the Fortune Line relates to time. The y-axis relates to emotions. The students' task is to identify where on the Fortune Line each card should be placed.

Once the students have been divided into pairs or small groups, they are then asked to sort the cards. Encourage the groups to share their strategy for sorting the cards with the whole class. They may decide to sort the cards chronologically or they may decide to sort by which cards they feel are relevant or irrelevant to answering the question.

Students are encouraged to place the cards on the graph. For each card placed, students must provide critical reasoning for their decisions. It is often useful to provide post-it notes for students to annotate their ideas and thinking.

Once all the cards have been plotted on the graph and each card has been analysed, ask your students to discuss the pattern that has emerged and what this tells us about how happy Anne Frank was. Invite groups to share their analysis with the whole class. Encourage each group to provide critical and constructive feedback.

## Questions to Promote Further Dialogue

- What evidence is there of Anne Frank experiencing happiness?
- Do you think Anne's parents were happy?
- Did Anne Frank experience happiness in spite of the reality of her situation?
- What can we learn about happiness from Anne Frank's diary?
- How does Anne's experience of happiness compare to your own?
- What influence did love have on Anne Frank's happiness?
- What influence did faith have on Anne Frank's happiness?
- Were Anne Frank's moments of happiness amplified or limited by the situation she found herself in?

## Adaptation

Fewer cards could be presented or more images used to deepen understanding.

## Extension

To add further challenge, ask your students to find their own quotations for the Fortune Line activity or provide a smaller selection.

To extend the activity, you could give your students blank cards and ask them to provide further events or quotations, which could explore the extent of Anne's happiness.

You could ask the students to create their own Fortune Line for a different character, for example, Peter Van Dann or Anne's mother.

Having explored this concept, you could ask your students to plan and write an essay in response to the key question.

# 4. CONSIDER THE LEARNING JOURNEY

At the end of the activity it is usual to encourage your students to review their learning journey and the thinking process they have engaged in throughout the session.

This can include reflection on the thinking that has taken place to this point, and a summary and conclusion of the new understanding reached.

Explicit reference to Learning Intentions and Success Criteria is a good starting point for this reflection, but it is also helpful to return to and re-examine some key questions:

- What do you understand about the concept of 'happiness'?
- How would you describe Anne Frank? Has your opinion of Anne changed?
- Do you think Anne Frank was happy?
- How did Anne's use of language help you understand her emotional state?
- How useful is Anne Frank's diary in helping us understand how people experience happiness during times of adversity?
- How does reflecting on other people's happiness impact on our own understanding of this concept?
- What will you remember about today's learning?
- What skills have you used during this lesson? When or where could you use them?

## Ideas for Transfer

Encourage your students to compile their own Fortune Line. A great comparison is to choose a weekday and a day during the weekend. Ask your students to evaluate how happy they are. This would include getting them to identify what makes them happy and what has a negative impact upon their behaviour or emotions.

Once students have analysed their Fortune Lines, a more in-depth study could take place around adolescent mental health. Areas to cover could include: bullying, family issues, friendships, eating patterns, sleep patterns, anger management, death and loss, and problems at school.

The focus would be on empowering the students to talk about their lives and to enable them to find solutions and answers to any concerns they may have.

Ask your students to explore other online diaries or blogs to explore how happiness is presented. They could write their own response to these entries or create their own web page.

Your students could collect and explore a range of current newspapers and magazines to determine how happiness is presented through the use of images, language, advertisements and articles. This could result in a collage to be presented to the rest of the class.

# WWW•EBI

# Why Was Winston Churchill's Speech Effective?

**KEY CONCEPT:** Rhetoric

**KEY SKILLS:** Analysing the main ideas of a primary or secondary source
Identifying the author's point of view in an informational text
Demonstrating an understanding of vocabulary specific to history/social studies
Citing textual evidence
Analysing an author's reasoning or claims in a text
Analysing ideas in diverse media formats
Evaluating a speaker's use of rhetoric

# Why Was Winston Churchill's Speech Effective?

**OVERVIEW:**

This lesson on 'Blood, Toil, Tears and Sweat' by Winston Churchill will enhance students' knowledge and understanding of the rhetorical devices and political intentions of this famous British Prime Minister. It would be useful for the students to be familiar with Winston Churchill and to know of his fame as an orator/speaker. Students need to know that this was his first speech as Britain's wartime leader and that it was essential for him to unite a nation facing the threat of Nazi Germany.

Students should listen to all, or some, of Winston Churchill's 'Blood, Toil, Tears and Sweat' speech. This is available online from a variety of sources.

**KEY CONCEPT:**

Rhetoric

**KEY WORDS:**

Speech, rhetoric, pathos, repetition, persuasion, slogan, power, effect, audience, speaker, delivery, message, appeal, rhetorical questions, unite, inspire, connect, motivate, convince, convey, oratory and soundbites.

**LEARNING INTENTION:**

To understand the persuasive impact of rhetorical devices in speech making.

**SUCCESS CRITERIA:**

We can do the following:

- Consider and define the concept of rhetoric.

- Name and identify rhetorical devices used in persuasive speech.

- Judge the strength and power of rhetorical devices.

- Analyse a speech and highlight the use of specific rhetorical devices.

- Determine what the most powerful elements of a speech are.

**STRATEGIES USED:**

Diamond Ranking x 2

# 1. IDENTIFY IMPORTANT CONCEPTS

Some of the key areas to investigate within and around the concept of 'rhetorical devices' are the following:

- A definition of rhetoric

- A definition of inspire, persuade, convince, motivate and convey

- The differences between verbal and written communication

- The conventions of writing versus the techniques of oratory

- Speaking with impact without vision versus speaking with impact with vision

- The evolution of speech making over time and the advent of new media

- Speech writing or making and audience

## Activity 1: Defining Terminology

Present your students with the list of these 10 rhetorical devices and strategies that speakers often use (found at the end of this Lesson). Ask them to look at the definition and example so that they begin to build a knowledge and understanding of these features of persuasive speech. As a preview to the rest of the lesson, you can ask them to explore a range of famous speeches to look for examples of these strategies being used.

**Download the full Device/ Strategy Chart at** http://resources.corwin.com/ learningchallengelessons

| Device or Strategy | Definition and Example |
|---|---|
| Ethos | Persuasive appeal of one's character – 'As a father and as a husband, I feel well qualified to say to you . . .' |
| Pathos | Persuasive appeal to emotion – 'Imagine for a moment an orphaned child, alone, sick . . .' |
| Logos | Persuasive appeal to logic – 'The scientific evidence is clear; the climate is changing and we must . . .' |
| Parallels or repetition | Repetition of the same, or similar, words, phrases or sentences to emphasise a point – 'we shall fight on the beaches, we shall . . .' |

This activity could be done as a Jigsaw so that students become experts and teachers of an individual device/strategy. This may help students for whom this amount of terminology is overwhelming.

# 2. CHALLENGE STUDENTS' UNDERSTANDING OF THE CONCEPT

The chart at the top of the next page gives some examples of cognitive conflict we expect students to experience.

| Opinion | Conflicting Opinion |
|---|---|
| A speaker can only persuade us of something we want to believe. | A speaker makes us think that we want to believe something. |
| Words are just words. | Words have power. |
| We can only be persuaded of the truth. | Many have believed the myth that the Great Wall of China is the only man-made object that can be seen from space, when actually there are many and the Great Wall is not one of them. |
| People know the truth when they hear it. | People once believed the world was square because this was the truth they were told. |
| We should be open-minded when we listen to people. | We should be cautious of the messages that people attempt to convey to us in speeches. |
| It's good to know the tricks speakers use to persuade and influence us. | Knowing how the magic works destroys our enjoyment of it. |
| Anyone can learn the rules of rhetoric and produce great speeches. | Many know the rules of rhetoric but only a few are renowned for their great speeches. |
| 'Sticks and stones may break my bones but words will never harm me.' | 'The pen is mightier than the sword.' |

### Questions for Challenge

- What is rhetoric?
- Does rhetoric always need to be persuasive?
- What makes a device in speech rhetorical?
- Why should we use rhetorical devices?
- Who decides if a rhetorical device is persuasive?
- To be persuaded, do you have to want to be persuaded?
- Has persuasion got anything to do with truth? What?
- What is the connection between being persuaded of something and fear?
- How are people persuaded of things?
- Could a good speaker persuade you to do something? How could they persuade someone else?
- Could a good speaker persuade you to believe in something? How could they persuade someone else?
- What is the difference between persuasion and coercion?
- What makes some speakers more inspirational and persuasive than others? Is it the person or the message?
- Could anyone write a good speech?
- Could anyone deliver a good speech?

- How can words have power if they are *just* words?

- How can we assess if words have been powerful or persuasive?

- When have you been affected by the power of words?

- How can you guard against the power of a speaker's message?

- What role does truth play in the success of rhetoric?

- Is it good to be open-minded to the messages in a speech?

- Is it good to be cynical about the motives or messages of a speech?

- If we know the rhetorical devices a good speaker uses to persuade us, does this change how we respond to the message?

- How could someone be persuaded into believing something that isn't true?

# 3. CONSTRUCT UNDERSTANDING

**Activity 2: Diamond Ranking**

Which is the most persuasive rhetorical device/strategy?

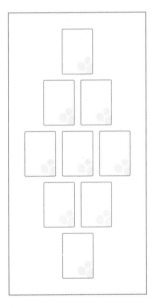

The Diamond Ranking strategy encourages active participation. It will help your students to prioritise the information, clarify their thoughts and create reasons and reflections. This needs to be a collaborative activity, so working in pairs is probably best.

Ask your students to focus on the following question:

**Which is the most persuasive rhetorical device?**

Ask your students to use the list of devices/strategies from **Activity 1**. Get them to place the one that they think is most persuasive at the top. The next two most persuasive should be placed underneath the first one, but side-by-side to each other to show they are thought of as 'second-equal'. After that, there are three third-equals, two fourth-equals and then the single least persuasive one at the bottom, as shown in the figure above. Your students should be left with one device/strategy that they haven't included in the ranking. They could identify this before or after the diamond is created.

| Device or Strategy | Example found in 'Blood, Toil, Tears and Sweat' speech – Winston Churchill |
|---|---|
| Ethos | |
| Pathos | |
| Logos | |
| Parallel or repetition | |
| Rhetorical questions | |
| Symbolism | |
| Slogan or catchphrase | |
| Allusion | |
| Analogy | |
| Metonomy | |

## Activity 3: Text Analysis

Ask your students to read and listen to the excerpt from Winston Churchill's 'Blood, Toil, Tears and Sweat' speech. Using the devices/strategies used in **Activity 1**, ask your students to identify the rhetorical devices and strategies that Churchill employed in delivering that speech. There is a table to help your students at the end of this Lesson and in the **Activity 3 resources**.

## Activity 4: Diamond Ranking

Once your students have listened to, read and carried out an analysis of the Churchill speech, ask them to now rank the rhetorical devices/strategies in terms of their power and/or persuasion. It is suggested that you adopt the same approach as you used in the previous Ranking activity (**Activity 2**). This time it is not expected that the 'Diamond' will consist of nine terms.

### Adaptation

Students could be given a smaller number of devices to find in **Activity 3**.

### Extension

To add more challenge to the **Activity 1** task, leave out some/all of the definitions for each strategy so students can fill in the gaps. Gaps could also be left in the strategy section of the table for students to complete.

Ask your students to explore the effects of each rhetorical device by creating a third column for the table from the **Activity 3 resources** with the heading, 'Effects on the reader'. To develop this into an essay, present your students with the following question:

**How does Churchill use rhetorical devices to persuade his audience?**

Use the rhetorical devices in an Odd One Out activity so your students can identify the differences and similarities between each strategy.

# 4. CONSIDER THE LEARNING JOURNEY

At the end of the activity it is worthwhile to encourage the students to review their learning journey and the thinking process they have participated in throughout the lesson.

This can consist of reflection on the thinking that has taken place by summarising and concluding on their new-found understanding.

Explicit reference to Learning Intentions and Success Criteria is a good starting point for this reflection, but it is also helpful to consider some of the following questions:

- What have you learnt about the strategies and devices that speakers and speech writers use in attempting to connect with and persuade an audience?
- What aspects of the lesson deepened your thinking?
- What aspects of the lesson helped you to confirm and/or reshape your knowledge and understanding of rhetoric?
- What would you like to find out more about?

- What will you take away from this lesson that you'll remember?
- Will you be able to use your understanding of this concept in other settings and other situations (i.e. is it transferable learning)?
- Why was Winston Churchill's speech effective?

## Ideas for Transfer

Using their understanding of rhetorical devices, encourage your students to explore other text types/genres to determine how persuasive language is used, for example: adverts, newspaper and magazine articles, news broadcasts, etc.

To demonstrate their understanding of rhetorical devices, ask your students to write their own speech using the same techniques as Winston Churchill.

Encourage your students to explore and analyse other political speeches, using the table of rhetorical devices.

| Device or Strategy | Definition and Example |
| --- | --- |
| Ethos | Persuasive appeal of one's character – 'As a father and as a husband, I feel well qualified to say to you . . .' |
| Pathos | Persuasive appeal to emotion – 'Imagine for a moment an orphaned child, alone, sick . . .' |
| Logos | Persuasive appeal to logic – 'The scientific evidence is clear; the climate is changing and we must . . .' |
| Parallels or repetition | Repetition of the same, or similar, words, phrases or sentences to emphasise a point – '**we shall** fight on the beaches, **we shall** fight on the landing grounds, **we shall** fight in the fields . . .' (Winston Churchill) |
| Rhetorical question | A question not to be answered but to encourage the listener to reflect on what the answer must be – 'How much longer must our people endure this injustice?' (Martin Luther King Jr) |
| Symbolism | When speeches utilise figures of speech, like metaphors, similes and allegory: 'All the world's a stage, And all the men and women merely players; They have their exits and their entrances . . .' (William Shakespeare) 'With him as the captain, the team could be headed for the rocks.' |
| Slogan or soundbite | Famous examples of these are: 'Ich bin ein Berliner.' (John F. Kennedy) 'The only thing we have to fear is fear itself.' (Franklin D. Roosevelt) |
| Allusion | A reference to another person, event or story – 'We struggle on carrying the weight of the world on our shoulders.' Reference to the Greek myth about Atlas who supported the world on his shoulders. |

*(Continued)*

(Continued)

| Device or Strategy | Definition and Example |
|---|---|
| Analogy | Making a comparison between things that are essentially alike. This is to persuade an audience that the logic of an idea should be accepted, like an established idea – 'Withdrawal of U.S. troops will become like salted peanuts to the American public; the more U.S. troops come home, the more will be demanded.' (Henry Kissinger) |
| Alliteration | Repetition of initial word sounds. It draws attention to an idea and fixes it in a listener's mind – 'Let us go forth to lead the land we love.' (John F. Kennedy) |

| Device or Strategy | Example found in 'Blood, Toil, Tears and Sweat' speech – Winston Churchill |
|---|---|
| Ethos | |
| Pathos | |
| Logos | |
| Parallels or repetition | |
| Rhetorical questions | |
| Symbolism | |
| Slogan or catchphrase | |
| Allusion | |
| Analogy | |
| Alliteration | |

# 'BLOOD, TOIL, TEARS AND SWEAT' – WINSTON CHURCHILL

13th May 1940

## Excerpt From His First Speech as Prime Minister to the House of Commons

. . . but it must be remembered that we are in the preliminary stage of one of the greatest battles in history, that we are in action at many points in Norway and in Holland, that we have to be prepared in the Mediterranean, that the air battle is continuous, and that many preparations have to be made here at home . . . I would say to the House as I said to those who have joined the government: '**I have nothing to offer but blood, toil, tears and sweat.**'

We have before us an ordeal of the most grievous kind. We have before us many, many long months of struggle and of suffering. You ask, what is our policy? I can say: It is to wage war, by sea, land and air, with all our might and with all the strength that God can give us; to wage war against a monstrous tyranny, never surpassed in the dark, lamentable catalogue of human crime. That is our policy. You ask, what is our aim? I can answer in one word: Victory – victory at all costs, victory in spite of all terror, victory, however long and hard the road may be; for without victory, there is no survival. Let that be realised; no survival for the British Empire, no survival for all that the British Empire has stood for, no survival for the urge and impulse of the ages, that mankind will move forward towards its goal. But I take up my task with buoyancy and hope. I feel sure that our cause will not be suffered to fail among men. At this time I feel entitled to claim the aid of all, and I say, 'come then, let us go forward together with our united strength.'

# WWW•EBI

EBI — Even Better If . . .

# What Was the Intent of President Reagan's Speech at Moscow State University in 1988?

**KEY CONCEPT:** Intent

**KEY SKILLS:** Analysing the main ideas of a primary or secondary source

Identifying the author's point of view in an informational text

Demonstrating an understanding of vocabulary specific to history/social studies

Citing textual evidence

Analysing an author's reasoning or claims in a text

Analysing ideas in diverse media formats

# What Was the Intent of President Reagan's Speech at Moscow State University in 1988?

## OVERVIEW:

This lesson will enhance students' knowledge and understanding of Ronald Reagan's speech and the wider historical and political context. It would be useful for students to be familiar with Ronald Reagan and his role as president prior to starting this activity and to have a copy of the speech available throughout.

## KEY CONCEPT:

Intent

## KEY WORDS:

Intent, purpose, objectives, speech, democracy, diplomacy, freedom, Cold War, economics, communism, socialism, Lenin, Marx, peace, revolution, progress, rhetoric, persuasion, promote, motivate, capitalism and the American Dream.

## LEARNING INTENTION:

To understand the intent of President Reagan's speech to Moscow State University.

## SUCCESS CRITERIA:

We can do the following:

- Define intent and what this means in terms of actions and behaviour.

- Identify the ways in which a speech can reveal the intent of a speaker.

- Find, identify and label specific examples of intentions within a speech made by Ronald Reagan.

- Judge the relative importance of individual intentions within Ronald Reagan's speech.

- Make connections between individual intentions to develop a greater understanding of overall intent.

- Assess what an understanding of intent means to our analysis of speeches and speakers.

## STRATEGIES USED:

Concept Target

Concept Map

Diamond Ranking

# 1. IDENTIFY IMPORTANT CONCEPTS

Some of the key areas to investigate within and around the concept of 'intent' are the following:

- A definition of intent
- The nature of intent compared with long-term purpose
- Self-interest, group interest, vested interest
- Agenda
- Philosophical beliefs
- Values
- Objectives
- Motivation
- Strategy
- Success criteria

# 2. CHALLENGE STUDENTS' UNDERSTANDING OF THE CONCEPT

Here are some examples of the cognitive conflict we expect your students to experience:

| Opinion | Conflicting Opinion |
|---|---|
| Intentions are very important. For example, an action only becomes bullying if there is the intent to bully. | Intentions are far less important than actions. For example, someone might intend to be nice to everyone they meet but if their actions do not follow suit, then their intentions are hollow. |
| Good intentions excuse bad outcomes. If a person or group has good intentions but the result is bad, then their good intentions counter the impact. If a hero rushes into battle against unsurmountable odds and dies the action is viewed as heroic rather than foolhardy. | Outcomes are felt more acutely than intentions. You may have good intentions from your point of view, but others see the action as so bad that the intention does not matter. The Nazi party's intent was to make Germany a great and powerful nation, but the good intention has been over-ridden by the impact of their actions. |
| Intent is the same as purpose. For example, both are related to a plan to achieve a certain end. | Purpose and intent are different. For example, the purpose of building a large shopping centre was to boost the local economy. It was not the intention to cause harm to the local environment in the process. |
| Intent means being determined to do (something). For example: 'The government was intent on achieving greater efficiency.' | Someone can intend to do something but not be determined enough to carry it out. For example, I intended to do my homework as soon as I got home from school but I was not determined enough to do it and got distracted by doing something else instead. |
| Our intentions are demonstrated in our behaviour. For example, if we intend to be a positive, proactive person the likelihood is that we will behave in that way. | Our behaviour often runs contrary to our intentions. For example, sometimes we have good intentions that are thwarted by events outside of our control. I couldn't meet my friend at the time I said I would because a traffic accident caused us to be late. |

## Questions for Challenge

- What do we mean by 'intent'?
- How do we know what intent is?
- What is the difference between intent and purpose?
- Does your purpose inform your intent?
- Do you need intent to have purpose?
- Are you born with intent?
- Does your purpose affect your behaviour?
- How does your intent change?
- What drives your intent?
- Is intention more important than action?
- Is your intent something you feel?
- How could you exist without having intent?
- Does everyone have intent?
- Should we always have intent in our day-to-day life?
- Do you have intent now?
- When is intent linked to need?
- How is intent linked to reward?
- How much does your understanding of someone's intentions impact on your understanding of the person?
- When is your intent not your own?
- Is working to serve someone else's intentions ever a bad thing?
- Is working to serve someone else's intentions always a sign of lack of control?
- What is the relationship between success and intent?
- What happens if your intent is not achieved?
- What or who influences your daily or minute-by-minute intent?
- Can you intend to do nothing? Is doing nothing an absence of intent?
- Is intent measurable? Do some people have more intent than others?
- Does your intent influence others?
- Is knowing why you want to do something more important than knowing how you are going to do it?
- Is your intent always aligned to your beliefs and values?
- Can we intend to do something that goes against our 'good' intentions?
- When can we do something and truly be able to say we didn't intend to do it?
- Is your intent always the same as your vision?
- How could your intent influence others?
- Can you persuade others to share and follow your intent?
- When should your intent be private and when should it be public?
- Is it easy to identify another person's intent?
- What would the world be like if we knew all of each other's intentions?
- How could knowing, naming and acknowledging your intent make you more successful?

# 3. CONSTRUCT UNDERSTANDING

## Activity 1: Concept Target

Ask your students to draw a Concept Target like the one shown below. In the inner circle they should write **Intent**. On separate small pieces of paper, your students should write all the ideas that relate to that concept or that have emerged through the dialogue process. There are some ideas below.

Students should take each idea in turn and decide whether it is a necessary characteristic of the concept (in which case they should move it to the inner circle), a probable characteristic (in which case they should put it in the outer circle), or an unrelated characteristic (in which case they should place it outside of the target area).

**Download the activity cards at http://resources.corwin.com/ learningchallengelessons**

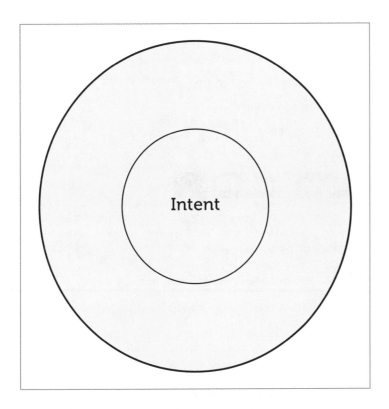

Intent

Some examples your students may wish to use to get them started are listed below and provided as **Activity 1 resource cards**:

- Purpose
- Something you want to achieve
- An idea you want to share
- Time wasting
- A need
- A goal
- An objective
- Someone else's instructions for you
- Success
- An agenda

- Selling something
- Showing-off
- A reward or pay-off
- Making/forming a plan
- Going along with everyone else
- Following somebody
- Waiting
- Being asleep
- Dreaming
- Breathing
- Persuasion
- Influence
- Consciously doing something
- Inadvertently doing something
- Clumsily doing something
- Badly doing something
- Unconsciously doing something

## Activity 2: Consider Reagan's Speech

**online resources**

**Download the text of President Reagan's speech at http://resources.corwin.com/ learningchallengelessons**

Allow students to read through President Reagan's speech (reproduced at the end of this Lesson), highlighting the parts that they find inspiring or persuasive, and identifying the key themes and intent of the speech.

Now allow the students to listen to President Reagan's speech.

- Do they think the speech is more inspiring and motivating when they listen to it as opposed to reading it?
- Do they understand the themes and intent of the speech more or less when listening to the orator as opposed to reading the text?

### Questions to Promote Further Dialogue

- Whose intent was Reagan attempting to serve in this and other speeches? His own or his nation's?
- Do you think Reagan revealed to the audience all of his intentions in relation to the Cold War with the USSR during the speech to Moscow State University?
- Which is the most powerful aspect of the speech, the passion or the intent?
- Simon Sinek believes that 'People don't buy what you do; they buy why you do it'. Do you agree?
- Do you think people bought into what Reagan did or why he did it?

## Activity 3: Concept Map

Introduce the idea of a Concept Map to your students focusing on the central question:

**What was the intent of President Reagan's speech at Moscow State University in 1988?**

Challenge them to make connections between President Reagan's intentions and to present logical inferences from his rhetoric.

Divide your students into small groups and present them with a large sheet of paper with the key question placed in the middle of the paper.

Provide each group with a set of blank cards or sticky notes, asking them to record any intentions or themes that they have identified within President Reagan's speech on the blank cards.

Your students should position or stick the cards to the paper and consider what links or connections they can identify between Reagan's various intentions. Each connection identified, and the reasoning and justification for it, should be written on a line between the intentions.

Invite each group to share their Concept Map with the whole class, encouraging them to provide critical and constructive feedback.

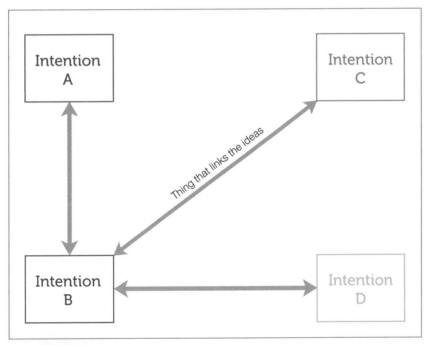

## Activity 4: Ranking

Working in small groups, your students should reconsider the intentions they've identified so far and narrow this list down to a top nine.

The Diamond Ranking structure should be used to evaluate and rank each of the nine intentions in order of importance. The intention of greatest importance should go at the top, with that of least importance at the bottom.

It is vital that students give reasons for their choices and that challenges and counter examples are encouraged. Your students should provide strong textual evidence to support their analysis of the speech.

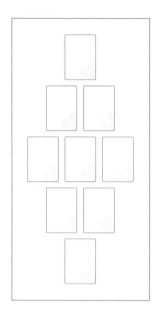

Examples of intentions for Diamond Ranking activity:

| To challenge communism. | To promote a notion of freedom. | To promote peace. |
|---|---|---|
| To end the Cold War. | To promote democracy. | To encourage freedom of religion. |
| To raise his profile. | To improve US–USSR relations. | To encourage economic progress. |
| To promote the American Dream. | To highlight his mistrust of the Soviet Union. | To encourage political change in the Soviet Union. |

### Adaptation

Students could be provided with examples of the intentions within the speech.

In the Concept Map activity, they may also benefit from one or two examples of connections.

### Extension

To extend the activity, you could ask students to cite textual analysis to support their ranking inferences and connections.

To add extra challenge, ask your students to answer the key question in essay form, using their Concept Maps and ranking for planning.

## 4. CONSIDER THE LEARNING JOURNEY

At the end of the activity it is usual to encourage your students to review their learning journey and the thinking process they have engaged in throughout the session.

This can include reflection on the thinking that has taken place to this point and a summary and conclusion of the new understanding reached.

Explicit reference to Learning Intentions and Success Criteria is a good starting point for this reflection, but it is also helpful to return to and re-examine some key questions:

- What do you understand about the concept of 'intent'?

- Do you have a greater understanding of President Reagan's intent in making this speech and, therefore, his core beliefs?

- What questions do you still have following today's lesson?

- How persuasive do you think President Reagan was?

- President Reagan delivered this speech in 1988. Is this speech out of date or is it still relevant in the 21st century?

- Does the American Dream still exist?

- Has your understanding of the speech increased as a result of your analysis?

- What will you remember about today's lesson?

- What skills have you used during today's lesson? When and where would you use these skills?

## Ideas for Transfer

Students could look at manifestos and speeches from current and former politicians and attempt to determine what the speaker or speech writer's intent is. Barack Obama's 'A More Perfect Union' would be a good example, as would Martin Luther King's 'I Have a Dream' speech or President J.F. Kennedy's inauguration speech.

Challenge your students to question what they think their intent is – in the short, medium and long term. Do they think their intent will change and when does our intent become our whole purpose in life?

Your students could be given an idea to speak to the class about. They can be asked to write and deliver their own speech, paying particular attention to identifying their intent throughout that speech. That intent might be to entertain, to inspire, to persuade, to explain or anything else that the students think is important.

Your students could watch archive video clips of other political speeches and attempt to identify the intent of the speaker.

# SPEECH AT MOSCOW STATE UNIVERSITY – RONALD REAGAN

31st May 1988

## Abridged Version of His Speech at Moscow State University

. . . Before I left Washington, I received many heartfelt letters and telegrams asking me to carry here a simple message – perhaps, but also some of the most important business of this summit – it is a message of peace and goodwill and hope for a growing friendship and closeness between our two peoples. . . .

But first I want to take a little time to talk to you much as I would to any group of university students in the United States. I want to talk not just of the realities of today, but of the possibilities of tomorrow. . . .

You know, one of the first contacts between your country and mine took place between Russian and American explorers. The Americans were members of Cook's last voyage on an expedition searching for an Arctic passage; on the island of Unalaska, they came upon the Russians, who took them in, and together with the native inhabitants, held a prayer service on the ice.

The explorers of the modern era are the entrepreneurs, men with vision, with the courage to take risks and faith enough to brave the unknown. These entrepreneurs and their small enterprises are responsible for almost all the economic growth in the United States. They are the prime movers of the technological revolution. In fact, one of the largest personal computer firms in the United States was started by two college students, no older than you, in the garage behind their home. Some people, even in my own country, look at the riot of experiment that is the free market and see only waste. What of all the entrepreneurs that fail? Well, many do, particularly the successful ones. Often several times. And if you ask them the secret of their success, they'll tell you it's all that they learned in their struggles along the way; yes, it's what they learned from failing. Like an athlete in competition, or a scholar in pursuit of the truth, experience is the greatest teacher. . . .

We are seeing the power of economic freedom spreading around the world. Places such as the Republic of Korea, Singapore, Taiwan have vaulted into the technological era, barely pausing in the industrial age along the way. Low-tax agricultural policies in the sub-continent mean that in some years India is now a net exporter of food. Perhaps most exciting are the winds of change that are blowing over the People's Republic of China, where one-quarter of the world's population is now getting its first taste of economic freedom. At the same time, the growth of democracy has become one of the most powerful political movements of our age. In Latin America in the 1970s, only a third of the population lived under democratic government. Today over 90 percent does. In the Philippines, in the Republic of Korea, free, contested, democratic elections are the order of the day. Throughout the world, free markets are the model for growth. Democracy is the standard by which governments are measured.

We Americans make no secret of our belief in freedom. In fact, it's something of a national pastime. Every four years the American people choose a new president, and 1988 is one of those years. At one point there were 13 major candidates running in the two major parties, not to mention all the others, including the Socialist and Libertarian candidates – all trying to get my job. About 1,000 local television stations, 8,500 radio stations, and 1,700 daily newspapers – each one an independent, private enterprise, fiercely independent of the government – report on the candidates, grill them in interviews, and bring them together for debates. In the end, the people vote; they decide who will be the next president. But freedom doesn't begin or end with elections.

The Lesson Ideas

Go to any American town, to take just an example, and you'll see dozens of synagogues and mosques – and you'll see families of every conceivable nationality, worshipping together. Go into any schoolroom, and there you will see children being taught the Declaration of Independence, that they are endowed by their Creator with certain unalienable rights – among them life, liberty, and the pursuit of happiness – that no government can justly deny; the guarantees in their Constitution for freedom of speech, freedom of assembly, and freedom of religion. Go into any courtroom and there will preside an independent judge, beholden to no government power. There every defendant has the right to a trial by a jury of his peers, usually 12 men and women – common citizens; they are the ones, the only ones, who weigh the evidence and decide on guilt or innocence. In that court, the accused is innocent until proven guilty, and the word of a policeman, or any official, has no greater legal standing than the word of the accused.

Go to any university campus, and there you'll find an open, sometimes heated discussion of the problems in American society and what can be done to correct them. Turn on the television, and you'll see the legislature conducting the business of government right there before the camera, debating and voting on the legislation that will become the law of the land. March in any demonstration, and there are many of them; the people's right of assembly is guaranteed in the Constitution and protected by the police. . . .

But freedom is more even than this. Freedom is the right to question and change the established way of doing things. It is the continuing revolution of the marketplace. It is the understanding that allows us to recognize shortcomings and seek solutions. It is the right to put forth an idea, scoffed at by the experts, and watch it catch fire among the people. It is the right to dream – to follow your dream or stick to your conscience, even if you're the only one in a sea of doubters. Freedom is the recognition that no single person, no single authority or government has a monopoly on the truth, but that every individual life is infinitely precious, that every one of us put on this world has been put there for a reason and has something to offer.

America is a nation made up of hundreds of nationalities. Our ties to you are more than ones of good feeling; they're ties of kinship. In America, you'll find Russians, Armenians, Ukrainians, peoples from Eastern Europe and Central Asia. They come from every part of this vast continent, from every continent, to live in harmony, seeking a place where each cultural heritage is respected, each is valued for its diverse strengths and beauties and the richness it brings to our lives. Recently, a few individuals and families have been allowed to visit relatives in the West. We can only hope that it won't be long before all are allowed to do so, and Ukrainian-Americans, Baltic-Americans, Armenian-Americans, can freely visit their homelands, just as this Irish-American visits his.

Freedom, it has been said, makes people selfish and materialistic, but Americans are one of the most religious peoples on Earth. Because they know that liberty, just as life itself, is not earned, but a gift from God, they seek to share that gift with the world. 'Reason and experience,' said George Washington, in his farewell address, 'both forbid us to expect that national morality can prevail in exclusion of religious principle. And it is substantially true, that virtue or morality is a necessary spring of popular government.' Democracy is less a system of government than it is a system to keep government limited, unintrusive; a system of constraints on power to keep politics and government secondary to the important things in life, the true sources of value found only in family and faith. . . .

I have often said, nations do not distrust each other because they are armed; they are armed because they distrust each other. If this globe is to live in peace and prosper, if it is to embrace all the possibilities of the technological revolution, then nations must renounce, once and for all, the right to an expansionist foreign policy. Peace between nations must be an enduring goal, not a tactical stage in a continuing conflict.

I've been told that there's a popular song in your country – perhaps you know it – whose evocative refrain asks the question, 'Do the Russians want a war?' In answer it says, 'Go ask that silence lingering in the air, above the birch and poplar there; beneath those trees the soldiers lie. Go ask my mother, ask my wife; then you will have to ask no more, "Do the Russians want a war?"' But what of your one-time allies? What of those who embraced you on the Elbe? What if we were to ask the watery graves of the Pacific, or the European battlefields where America's fallen were buried far from home? What if we were to ask their mothers, sisters, and sons, do Americans want war? Ask us, too, and you'll find the same answer, the same longing in every heart. People do not make wars, governments do. And no mother would ever willingly sacrifice her sons for territorial gain, for economic advantage, for ideology. A people free to choose will always choose peace.

Americans seek always to make friends of old antagonists. After a colonial revolution with Britain we have cemented for all ages the ties of kinship between our nations. After a terrible civil war between North and South, we healed our wounds and found true unity as a nation. We fought two world wars in my lifetime against Germany and one with Japan, but now the Federal Republic of Germany and Japan are two of our closest allies and friends.

Some people point to the trade disputes between us as a sign of strain, but they're the frictions of all families, and the family of free nations is a big and vital and sometimes boisterous one. I can tell you that nothing would please my heart more than in my lifetime to see American and Soviet diplomats grappling with the problem of trade disputes between America and a growing, exuberant, exporting Soviet Union that had opened up to economic freedom and growth. . . .

Is this just a dream? Perhaps. But it is a dream that is our responsibility to have come true.

Your generation is living in one of the most exciting, hopeful times in Soviet history. It is a time when the first breath of freedom stirs the air and the heart beats to the accelerated rhythm of hope, when the accumulated spiritual energies of a long silence yearn to break free. . . .

We do not know what the conclusion of this journey will be, but we're hopeful that the promise of reform will be fulfilled. In this Moscow spring, this May 1988, we may be allowed that hope: that freedom, like the fresh green sapling planted over Tolstoy's grave, will blossom forth at least in the rich fertile soil of your people and culture. We may be allowed to hope that the marvellous sound of a new openness will keep rising through, ringing through, leading to a new world of reconciliation, friendship, and peace.

Thank you all very much and *da blagoslovit vas gospod* – God bless you.

The Lesson Ideas

# WWW•EBI

## WWW – What Worked Well . . .

## EBI – Even Better If . . .

# REFERENCES

# REFERENCES

Mercer, N. (2000) *Words and Minds: How We Use Language to Think Together*. London: Routledge.

Nottingham, J.A. (2017) *The Learning Challenge*. Thousand Oaks, CA: Corwin.

Nottingham, J.A, Nottingham J. and Renton, M. (2017) *Challenging Learning through Dialogue*. Thousand Oaks, CA: Corwin.

Russell, B. (1975 [1933]) 'The Triumph of Stupidity'. In *Mortals and Others, Volume I: American Essays 1931–1935*. Abingdon, UK: Routledge.

Vygotsky, L.S. (1978) *Mind in Society: The Development of Higher Psychological Processes*. Cambridge, MA: Harvard University Press.

Wegerif, R. (2002) 'The Importance of Intelligent Conversations', *Teaching Thinking*, Autumn, Imaginative Minds Ltd, Birmingham.

Yeats, W.B. (1996 [1919]) 'The Second Coming'. In R.J. Finneran (ed.), *The Collected Poems of W.B. Yeats* (Rev. edn). New York: Scribner.

# PHOTOCOPIABLE MASTERS

In the following section you will find blank photocopiable masters that will act as frames or graphics to support the activities within the lesson plans.

Where appropriate, you will find guidance at the bottom of the photocopiable sheet for how to scale these items to enable students to achieve 'best fit' with activity cards.

Strongly Agree

Learning Challenge Lessons, Secondary English Language Arts

OPINION CORNERS:

Agree

Disagree

Strongly Disagree

# DIAMOND 9 RANKING:

**Diamond 9 Ranking Frame**
for visual reference

Challenging LEARNING    Learning Challenge Lessons, Secondary English Language Arts

# PYRAMID RANKING:

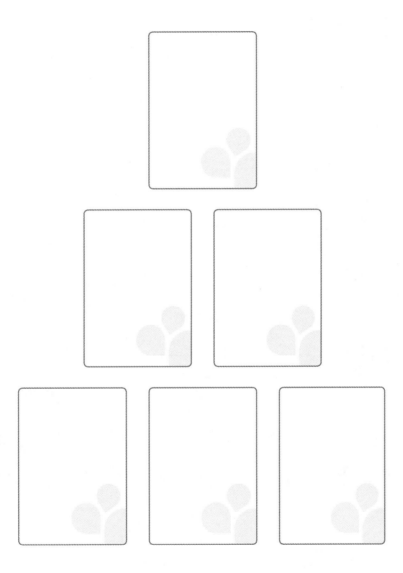

**Pyramid Ranking Frame**
for visual reference

# LINEAR RANKING:

**Linear Ranking Frame**
for visual reference

# VENN DIAGRAM:

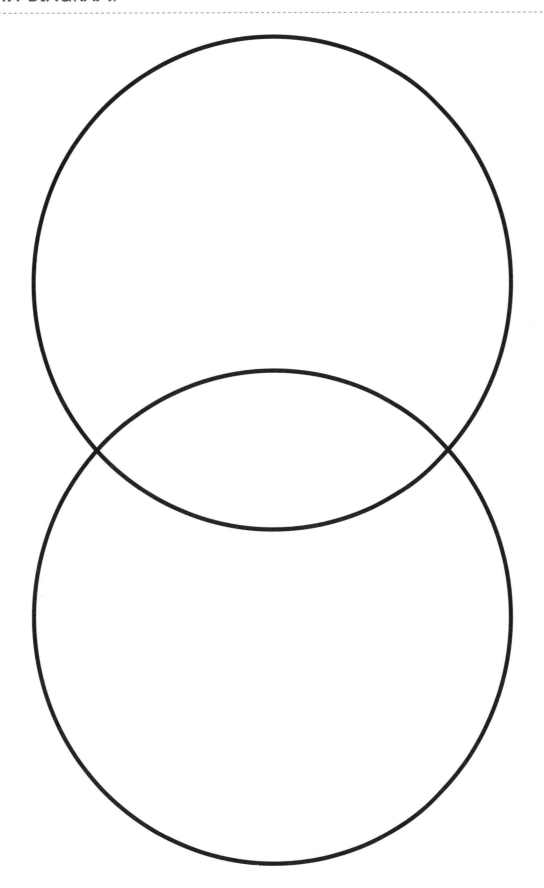

# BLANK AXIS FOR FORTUNE LINE AND LIVING GRAPH:

Challenging LEARNING

Learning Challenge Lessons, Secondary English Language Arts

# CONCEPT CORNERS:

Examples or contexts where the concept applies:

Examples of related ideas or associations:

Examples of phrases or sentences where the concept is used:

Examples of words or phrases of similar or opposite meaning:

# CONCEPT TARGET:

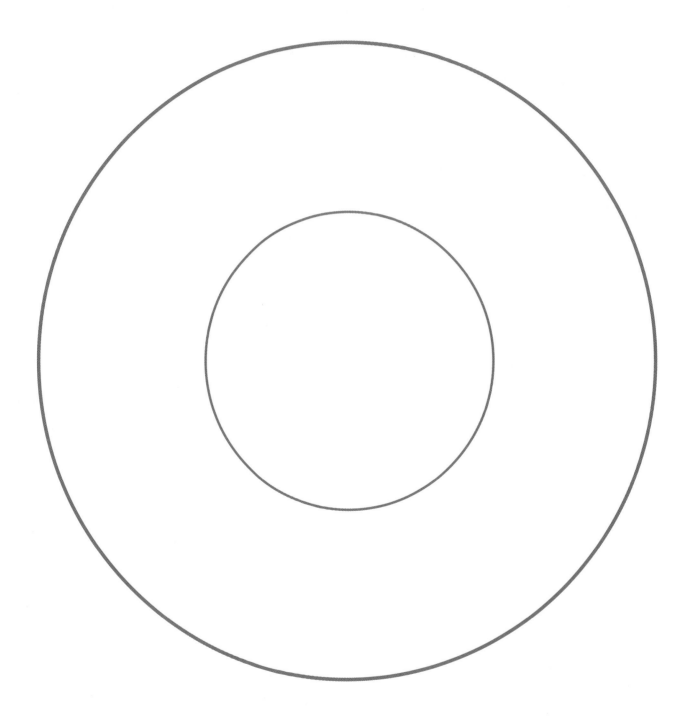

# INDEX

# Helping educators make the
## *greatest impact*

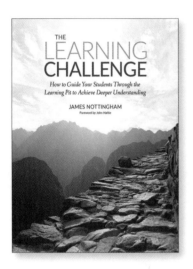

### James Nottingham
Dive into the Learning Pit and show students how to promote challenge, dialogue, and a growth mindset.

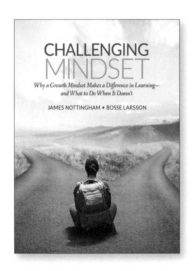

### James Nottingham and Bosse Larsson
Create the right conditions for a growth mindset to flourish in your school and your students.

### The Learning Challenge Dry-Erase Poster
### James Nottingham
An easy way to help document students' journeys through the Learning Challenge.

### Jill Nottingham and James Nottingham
Twenty compelling Learning Challenge lessons provide teachers with everything needed to facilitate thoughtful, rigorous, dialogue-driven challenges for elementary school students around topics of current importance.

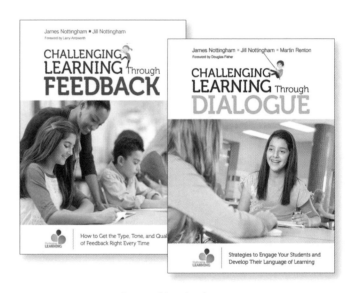

### James Nottingham, Jill Nottingham, and Martin Renton
Use feedback and classroom discussions to teach good habits of thinking and learning.

corwin.com

Corwin books represent the latest thinking from some of the most respected experts in PreK–12 education. We are proud of the breadth and depth of the books we publish and the authors we partner with in our mission to better serve educators and students.

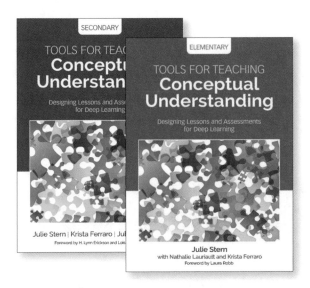

**Julie Stern, Nathalie Lauriault, Krista Ferraro, and Juliet Mohnkern**

Help students uncover conceptual relationships and transfer them to new problems.

**Guy Claxton**

Powerful resources to help teachers understand how "every lesson, every day" shapes the way students see themselves as learners.

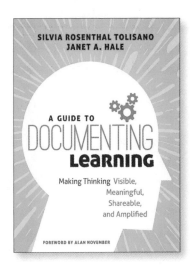

**Silvia Rosenthal Tolisano and Janet A. Hale**

Facilitate student-driven learning and help teachers reflect on their own learning and classroom practice.

**John Antonetti and Terri Stice**

Research and strategies educators need to design engaging, powerful learning tasks.

A SAGE Publishing Company

**CORWIN HAS ONE MISSION:** to enhance education through intentional professional learning.

We build long-term relationships with our authors, educators, clients, and associations who partner with us to develop and continuously improve the best evidence-based practices that establish and support lifelong learning.